PLAYBACK

PLAYBACK
Ronald Hayman

Horizon Press **New York**

First published in the United States in 1974 by
Horizon Press

Copyright © 1973 by Ronald Hayman

Library of Congress Cataloging in Publication Data

Hayman, Ronald
  Playback.

  1. Theater.   I. Title.
PN2189.H3   1973b   792'.092'2   74-4373
ISBN 0-8180-0506-8

CONTENTS

DAVID STOREY

Like Günter Grass and David Mercer, David Storey was an art student before he became a writer. Probably a training in a field where the whole work of art can make an instantaneous impact on the viewer produces habits and inclinations which survive when the artist moves on to writing – producing artifacts which work quite differently on the reader or audience, unrolling in front of him a series of separate impacts. While the play-in-performance contains more visual elements than the novel – set, lighting, costumes, faces, bodies and movements all contributing as directly as the playwright's words to the audience's experience – the novel can accommodate very much more verbal description than the play, and there is a more direct connection between the writer's words and the pictures that form in the reader's mind. There are no other personalities, pictures or ideas to get in the way.

David Storey has said 'I feel I'm more a novelist than a playwright. The sentimental attachment is always to a novel. But I think the thing is dead on its feet. The ones that succeed rely more intensely on the visual conception of what's going on, largely because the social conception has virtually disappeared. The nineteenth century novel really was a novel of manners – the way a man dressed, for instance, could tell you a great deal about him and his position, his world, his temperament – whereas this is no longer so. Today there is no kind of cohesive social gesture which illustrates or opens up a wide aspect of society, which in a way disarms the novel itself. So you're left with either the interior element – endless subjective novels – or what we're going for in this country, imitation novels, rather like Angus Wilson. Using an old conception of a novel and trying to animate it with new but in the end basically conventional material.'

To some extent he had the feeling of going to the novel

because there was nothing else to go to. 'I find what the novel means to me, its significance, is very strong, but I don't know how one can express it strongly any more. All that prose somehow gets in the way. Unless it is invested with a tremendous intellectual energy from someone like Bellow. Apart from that I can't see how a novel can acquire a new kind of unity with all these disconnected bits and pieces. The social bond has gone now. Either you go back to writing – like most of my contemporaries – conventional nineteenth century novels or just write purely subjectively, an esoteric piece of prose.'

The attraction, then, of drama might lie partly in the refuge it provides from 'all that prose'. The son of a miner, he had been a bus-conductor and a footballer – amongst many other things – before he started writing novels, and he wrote about seven before he had any success.

'I think *Sporting Life* was about the eighth novel I'd written and I got so tired of trying to get them published that after *Sporting Life* had been turned down about eight times, I thought "Well I've got nothing left here, perhaps I'm really a dramatist". I was then teaching in Islington and during one half term I took time off and wrote a play. I didn't feel I'd got very far, and left it and went on with *Sporting Life*. Two years later it was published. Then there was a backlog of novels, two of which came out during the next three years, *Flight into Camden and Radcliffe*. Then I set to work on another novel which took me about four years to write and got nowhere. In 1966 a boy who had worked at the Royal Court wrote to me to say he'd seen a copy of my play at the theatre some years before – and that he had taken over the Traverse Theatre in Edinburgh, and would I mind if he did the play there. Rather as a result of the Traverse production the Court did a production of it the following summer.'

It was in 1958 that he had written the play, which he called *To Die with the Philistines*. Then in 1960, when he was twenty-seven, his first two novels *This Sporting Life* and *Flight into Camden* were both published and both won important prizes. In 1964 there were plans for a production of his play at the Royal Court, and he did more work on it, changing the title to *The Restoration of Arnold Middleton*, but it was not actually staged until November 1966, when Gordon MacDougall directed it at the Traverse, Edinburgh, with David

Collings as Arnold and Marian Diamond as his wife, Joan. The production at the Court followed in July 1967, directed by Robert Kidd, with Jack Shepherd as Arnold and Eileen Atkins as Joan (a part taken over by June Barry when the production transferred to the Criterion at the end of August). Harold Hobson hailed it as 'the best first play produced by the English Stage Company since *Look Back in Anger.*'

All David Storey's subsequent plays – *In Celebration* (1969) *The Contractor* (1969) *Home* (1970) and *The Changing Room* (1971) had been directed by Lindsay Anderson, whose first contact with Storey came when they worked together on the film *This Sporting Life.* 'We spent about two and a half years, I think, making that. It was the first time Lindsay had directed a feature film, it was the first time I'd written one, and the first time Karel Reisz had produced one, and the first time Richard Harris had ever taken the lead. So it was a very exploratory period for all of us, really, and I think we reached an understanding through what might be called the nightmare of making that particular film.

'I was very reluctant to script the book as it was and really wanted to use it as a starting-off point, and I think Lindsay's tendency with actors and with writers is to let them have their head, and if what happens is real, then he accepts it, and if it's not, he'll say so, rather than determine beforehand what's required – I mean that's the objective. It's an empirical way of working. So I can imagine some actors at the beginning of a production feeling perhaps at a loss as to what's going on; gradually however a shape evolves – organically – from both them and the material, determining precisely what structure is there and controlling it, saying yes or no. With a play Lindsay accepts the text and then that's it basically. With a film too I think he works very closely from a script, whereas other directors tend to use a script merely as a stepping-off ground and frequently abandon it. I think *This Sporting Life* was something of a special case because neither of us knew what the other was like or really understood the material in terms of making a film of it. It wasn't until Richard Harris appeared on the scene that there was any kind of real catalyst. His response to it was organic, a complete emotional commitment. My own attitude to the material was one of detachment. I didn't want to go through it all again. I think Richard's great value was to bring us back to the material of the book. This is what we responded to. And being able to express that clearly and directly in a way we could get hold of and work from.

'Richard had been identifying with the book because when Lindsay went out to see him in the South Seas when he was making *Mutiny on the Bounty* – he'd spent six months there filming – he'd learnt great chunks of the book off by heart. It's not a book anyone would particularly care to learn by heart.'

The plans to produce *The Restoration of Arnold Middleton* in 1964 originated out of Anderson's asking Storey whether he had ever thought of writing for the stage, but what actually triggered a very productive period of play-writing was the experience of finally seeing *The Restoration of Arnold Middleton* in performance. 'And the plays really came out after that. Having been bogged down with a novel which I'd worked at obsessively for three or four years, when *Arnold Middleton* came, it offered an alternative – just seeing it on the stage resulted in several more plays popping out, six or seven. We're gradually working through them at the moment. *The Contractor* was written immediately after *Arnold Middleton* had been on at the Court, and when I'd finished *The Contractor* I was struck by the image of the white table at the end, a white metalwork table which is left on the stage. I went back to the novel and perhaps two or three weeks later sat down one morning and thought of the table sitting by itself and thought "Well that's the beginning of something" and wrote a description of a metalwork table sitting by itself on a stage with two white chairs, bringing on a chap after a little while – somebody has to appear – who sits down, followed a moment later by someone else – he can't sit there alone too long. It really began like that, and it was written about the same time. *In Celebration* was also written either during or just before – in a few days. I wrote two plays called *Home,* and this is the better of the two, I believe. And then I went back to the novel.'

The facility for writing as quickly as this was obviously acquired through working on the novels. Some of the plays grow directly out of the novels. *The Contractor* grew out of *Radcliffe,* where the two main characters get jobs with a firm of tent contractors which, like the one in the play, employs a great many social misfits. Some of the workmen even have the same names in both novel and play. But for David Storey dramatic dialogue is something generically different from dialogue in fiction. 'I think they're essentially different. I don't think you can transpose literary dialogue into dramatic dialogue. It has to have a different dimension. In a novel it's more leisurely. It's a different conception of what dialogue has to do and what it means.'

One of the key differences between them is that in the novel the reader need not be particularly aware – unless the writer wants him to be – of characters who are present during a scene but not contributing to it by speaking or reacting. In the theatre everyone on stage needs somehow to be participating in whatever is going on. This is something Storey learned from Lindsay Anderson's reaction to some scenes he wrote for *This Sporting Life*.

'We discussed them and he said "Yes that's good, but what are these other three characters doing while these two are talking?" In my naïve literary fashion, I'd shoved them to the back of the room. In a novel you tend to forget the silent characters while you get on with the active ones. If no-one speaks for five minutes it doesn't matter, whereas you can't have people fidgeting around on a stage waiting to come out with a line whenever it's required. It was only then I appreciated that when you're actually watching dialogue, it has to have a completely different inner dynamic, that everyone has to be engaged in some way or other even if they are passive – they've got to be engaged in a way that's just as important, as informative, as the people who are talking. The moment you accept that that's essential, the material begins to create itself. The moment someone is hanging around doing nothing, you realize something's gone wrong somewhere, the play's losing its momentum, and you've got to think carefully about what's happening. Writing dialogue's so easy you can go on for pages and pages, pouring the stuff out, and it's all interesting stuff to read, but to ask actors to give it cohesion is a different matter. With a film it's perhaps even more important, because it's got to be much briefer and tighter.'

But though it may sometimes have let him down, David Storey had always had a good flair for picturing what might be happening between the actors speaking his dialogue. Thanks partly perhaps to his experience of painting, he could form in

his mind a three-dimensional image of how the interrelation-
ships might be brought to physical realization. 'When I went
back to *Arnold Middleton* and read it through, there were
passages where it broke down for the reason I've mentioned;
a couple of characters had been shoved back while the others
got on with what they had to do. When I rewrote it, I had
that kind of discipline much more consciously in mind.'

But the essential quality of his work comes, above all, from
the characteristic balance he achieves between the literary
and the visual. Structure is particularly important in his plays:
their overall shape is almost sculptured. *The Contractor* takes
its form from the erection and dismantling of the tent. After
starting with an empty stage, we see the tent being put up
and then being prepared for the wedding breakfast. This takes
place in the interval between Act II and Act III, and the lights
next go up on the chaos of empty bottles, dirty glasses and
plates, damaged decorations and overturned furniture that the
wedding guests have left. This is cleared up, the tent is taken
down and we end, as we began, with an empty stage. *In
Celebration* also centres on a celebration meal, which again
takes place in the interval. The play is about a family reunion
occasioned by the fortieth wedding anniversary of a coalminer and his wife. As the play begins, one of their three sons
is arriving in the heavily-furnished living-room of their home.
The other two arrive, the conversation between sons, parents
and neighbours produces a series of insights into the lives they
are all leading, and we see that those of the parents and neighbours have changed very little since the sons, now all in their
thirties, were children. They stay overnight but leave in the
morning. The excitement over, the parents resume their lives.

In *The Contractor* a great deal of cutting was done but in
The Changing Room the focus is wider, taking in all
thirteen members of a professional rugby team, the cleaner of
the changing room, the trainers, the referee and the club
manager and chairman. Again, though the play is about the
people, its shape – like that of Wesker's *The Kitchen* – is
determined by the place, and though the place (unlike the tent
in *The Contractor*) has a continuing existence both before and
after the action, it comes to life only at the time of the game,
and what we see is constructed around two busy climaxes,
with the players changing first into their rugby clothes and,

later, out of them. Again the main climax of action – the game itself – is excluded from the play, and again we begin and end very quietly, this time with the old cleaner, who never watches the game but whose life centres on the changing room. The wooden benches, the clothes-pegs, the towels, the rugby boots, socks, singlets and shorts, and the physical actions, including massage and the referee's inspection, contribute to the life of the play on almost exactly the same level as the words.

Because place, objects and actions are so very important in Storey's plays, especially *The Contractor* and *The Changing Room*, some people have the impression that Lindsay Anderson is involved in the preparation of the text, but he is not. All the plays produced so far were written before Anderson did his first production of a Storey play – *In Celebration* in 1969. 'I'd say the quality he brings to them is of clarity, directness – allowing them to live their own life, and not imposing an interpretation on them which either is alien, or is more or less his own, or even the author's. He allows the material to speak for itself and doesn't accentuate one interpretation at the expense of others.'

The close working relationship with Anderson has been extremely valuable to Storey. 'It's the kind of relationship you tend not to explore, because the more you look at it, the more mechanical it might become. I think broadly we both start off from opposite positions. Lindsay starts off from a kind of Tolstoyan viewpoint, a total picture of whatever you're doing, whereas I'm inclined to start off from a detail and work up towards a complete picture – all being well. In terms of actual work we arrive at a common ground from opposite corners. We never actually discuss what it's all about. The whole thing works without any kind of exposition beforehand. It's really an intuitive response.

'In terms of cutting, this is very useful. I write the plays and then leave them for three or four months and then take them out and read them through again, and if it strikes a bell anywhere, I type them out and cut them down but leave pieces in whenever I'm unsure. I find Lindsay's good at placing the overall structure and indicating the bits which really do impede it. Particularly with *In Celebration*, where there was a formidable amount of material: cutting gave it a much clearer definition.'

In *The Contractor* a great deal of cutting was done but in fact most of the cuts were restored in rehearsal. 'The play was all conceived in terms of work. On the page it seems that nothing's going on – an author's self-indulgence – but in rehearsal we gradually put it all back, with a little bit more besides.

'Each play, I suppose, is different to that extent. *In Celebration* is a more literary play. It's basically people sitting in a room talking about themselves and other people. Although the effect, if it works, is a theatrical one, you'd say its antecedents were more literary than theatrical, and therefore as a text it's much more amenable to cutting; whereas *The Contractor*'s such a physical thing that you can't really relate the text to it directly. The conception is more theatrical. I suppose one learns from all this. In *The Changing Room*, for example, which technically is a very difficult play to do, with a great deal of physical action which has to be carefully co-ordinated, we didn't have to remove a line. Apart from an odd word, to let an actor leave, or to facilitate his entry, there were no additions either.'

Do they happen in very different ways to you – the different kinds of conception?

'They tend to pop out at the same time, so it's really a question of moving from one to the other. They're all, in a way, traditional plays because they all have one set, one environment, and everything happens within it. In the past I've tried to write plays where there was a constant change of environment – Shakespeare's change every minute, don't they? – rather like a novel, where you move from one event to another, but I found – until recently – the unity of one place was all I could manage. Given a set at the beginning, I found it terribly hard to get out of it. A play I've completed recently – *Cromwell* – achieves a certain success, I think, in this direction.'

To say that the plays have become less literary and more visual as Storey has developed would be an over-simplification, but whereas *Home*, for instance, grew out of an image, *The Restoration of Arnold Middleton* started out of an anecdote – 'Which again, is literary. I tend to start novels from anecdotes, and plays from a first line, which is followed by a second. I think *Arnold*, in that sense, is pretty close to a novel. It exists in its own terms perhaps as a play, but when I watch it, I get the feeling it's written by someone who should really write novels.

'Similarly with *In Celebration*. I think this reveals itself particularly in one of the characters, played in the original production by Brian Cox, who has to sit in silence for virtually the whole play, not because the author doesn't think he's important, but because he hasn't got anything to say, or if he has, he can't express it. Someone who'd been an actor or brought up in a theatrical tradition would never have written a character like that, knowing how difficult, technically, it is for an actor to play that part. He has to fill it with a kind of energy which is totally static, and yet he must never be boring. John Gielgud had a similar task before him in *Home* with Harry, with all his Oh yeses and his silences and his incapacity to say anything very clearly. Although once it is achieved it is very moving and perhaps even eloquent in its own way, its roots are essentially literary. Now I know more about the theatre, I would never dare to write parts like that again, making that kind of demand on an actor. . . . They're all plays of understatement in a way and if you don't get what they're understating, then you've really had it, because there's nothing great going on on the surface. It's all got to be going on in the audience's mind, particularly with *Home*.'

The effectiveness of *In Celebration* also depends largely on how far it succeeds in getting the action going in the audience's mind. It seems as though the play is leading towards a big showdown between mother and eldest son, but this never comes. 'I thought the point of the play was that there was no kind of conventional confrontation. In a way the explosion has already taken place off or outside or away, and this is the aftermath. If you compare it - however tentatively - with Ibsen in terms of approaching psychological realities, Ibsen is writing about a time in history before the explosion has occurred, the bomb is festering away inside and eventually goes off. With *In Celebration*, it's not a question of stripping off hypocrisies, deceits and complacencies, but of asking what do you do with the people afterwards - and *are* they really deceit and hypocrisy and complacency? Aren't the parents, for instance, in *In Celebration* more "real", less pretentious and more effective as people than their three so-called emancipated sons? The truth of the play perhaps lies in *that* confrontation, rather than the one that is seemingly avoided on the surface.

'I would have said that the play could only have been written fifty or a hundred years after Ibsen in that sense. There really is no stripping away any more. The illusions in that sense have gone. People stick to the lying. The bomb is there and we no longer need the explosion, the ripping out of the heart and head. It really is a question of soldiering on, or of compromising, or forgiving, as the play suggests at the end. I don't know whether this is too literary or not, an author's self-indulgence. If it is, then the play is a failure.

'I think *The Contractor*'s a similar case of a deliberate withdrawal from drama in that sense. Again, all the confrontations that could take place there, are, if you like, skilfully avoided, because the actual conception of the play is directed towards that end rather than explosion and revelation.'

Home in some sense arrives at a point towards which the earlier plays had been striving. *The fact of non-confrontation is made integral to the conception and to the nature of the characters. They have to be people who don't, who can't confront what there is to confront, and that's the subject, isn't it?*

'That may be true. I think *Home*'s limitations are there for everyone to see. Whereas with the other plays I feel there is a lurking ambition to broaden the conception and to set the limits a bit higher than they have been set. Perhaps because it was written so quickly, within a couple of days, *Home* doesn't try to shift its premisses and is probably more of an entity.'

When he started writing it he had not decided where the metalwork table was, or what the characters were going to be like. 'It was only when the ladies came on that I began to suspect they were in a mental home and not where I thought they were, in a hotel. When the ladies appear there's this terrible reversal of roles – the women behave like men and the men more like women. It was when they began to refer explicitly to their various ailments that I realized they were slightly unstable. I think that's where the reviews did a disservice to the play in saying that it was about a madhouse. It's a given premiss, if you like, but in fact it's not the material of the play itself, and to say it's a mental home is a way of distancing the audience from the play. It isn't just that it diminishes the play and the conception, making it a special case, but it sets you away from the emotion, from the suffering; whereas the characters, I would think, are those you might meet in the street any day.

'I wouldn't think any of the characters are actually insane. They could quite as easily have been outside as inside, I feel. In fact, when we did the play at Brighton and stayed at these terrible hotels, there were thousands of them all round us. You know, the same dialogue. And when Sir John and Sir Ralph stopped rehearsing, you were never quite sure whether they were talking or rehearsing. There is a sort of disclaimer really when it becomes firmly a play about a mental home. It makes the audience feel apart from it – "These people are mad and we're not mad. How extraordinary the things that mad people do!" I think people in mental homes in real life are slightly different from this, just from their aspect. You'd never find anyone as convivial as that in a mental home. In fact most of them – when they aren't actively deranged – are passive and silent.'

Storey's speed in writing plays is all the more remarkable when compared with the time he has invested in the novels. He has toiled at these almost like a miner, laboriously digging them out, bit by bit, from deep underground. A novel called *A Temporary Life* which has not yet been published, took two years to write, and *Pasmore*, which appeared in 1972, was a by-product of a much larger novel he had been working at for seven years. 'I have a strong resistance to reading anything I've written until I absolutely have to. I was prepared to spend four or five years on this particular novel. It was one that I wanted to do when I was very young, and this was a conception I'd built up to slowly through *Sporting Life* and *Camden* and *Radcliffe*, with varying degrees of success. Then I sat down and wrote it but found when I came to read it, it didn't work. It must be seven years since I began and I'm still writing it. *Pasmore* is a kind of interim statement. I've written several novels on or around this theme. Three of them are virtually – not the same novel, but they involve the same situation and characters in three different conceptions. The great bulk of work from which they are detached is the main thing, and in a way the plays stem from that – little shoots off the side.'

The original theme of this novel was the split in Storey's life which became evident when he was a student, spending the week trying to paint (following his training at the Slade School) and playing professional rugby at the week-ends, in Yorkshire. 'I couldn't see any connection between the reality of the one thing, a very rough and hard game played for money, and the terrible reality of the other, a completely introverted event calling on – as I then thought – great powers of self-absorption. The novel I wanted to write was about a character in whom this feeling of sub-division had been resolved, where these two elements were in some sort of equilibrium. The division between those who can make society work for them and those who can't was so marked in my life at that time that I felt driven into writing about it.

'This division was not just one of temperament but could be reflected in society as well. In the coal-mining area I came from, an artist was a fairly suspect fellow doing something for no apparent purpose and with no tangible reward – here were these men working down the pit all week and providing funds for people like me to go and paint pictures, which *they* could do at week-ends, if they wanted, as well as work. I felt this division both within my own family and the world around – and the corresponding pressure was to find some kind of resolution. *This Sporting Life* was a first attempt at writing about a man who could make society work but not much else. *Flight into Camden* was an attempt to write about someone who had an intuitive response to life and not much else, who couldn't really get on with people. *Radcliffe* was where these two characters were brought together. *Radcliffe* was the intuitive outcast, with something of an artistic temperament, and the other character was a man with a good appetite for life, a sort of blindness to life and who got on with it, but felt that something else was missing. This large novel was an attempt to bring the two elements together within the life of one individual. I suppose that theme is in the plays, certainly in Arnold Middleton, the chap who quietly goes mad while he maintains a kind of charade till he can't relate to anything. In *In Celebration* there's an attempt, I believe, to break it up. That was the most deliberately written of the plays. Beforehand I decided there would be three arguments in the play. One was the ascetic, silent temperament; there would also be the latently revolutionary one; the third man who, rather like Harold Wilson, says this is the best of all possible worlds and you've got to make a go of it.

'I suppose, looking back over all this work, I tend to see it – not wholly for defensive reasons – as a kind of failure. I was very much aware in the past, for instance, of trying to match one kind of life with another – an inner life with an outer; or a working-class life and its instincts with a middle-class life and its urges towards reason and the status quo – and I couldn't in the end, or I can't now, see any resolution. I've had enough time and opportunity to see that there are great themes that can be expressed in literature and drama, yet – perhaps through a romantic addiction to the role of the artist, perhaps through a simple lack of talent – I've never quite made it. I still see it all in working-class terms, as competition, like a runner trying to get some impossible record; or a boxer fighting for a championship: I write every day – in one sense – in order to keep 'fit'. I'm not sure it's the best thing to do, or even required. A coalminer puts in his shift each day; an athlete trains to maintain a certain consistency and standard, as a stepping-off board to something higher. To ask me to take a day off from writing is like asking a prospector to give up – if only temporarily – the rights to his claim, when it might *just* be that day that fate has destined him to dig up a kingsize nugget. On the whole he knows, doesn't he, the chances are against it?'

Storey may regard himself – perhaps not unduly – as a pessimist; but it's interesting that there is one writer who, for him, typifies a successful synthesis between the two kinds of life. Günter Grass and he have more than an art school background in common: they have both been trying energetically – as very few recent English writers have tried—to work both as novelists and in the theatre. Storey feels a very warm admiration for Grass.

'When I met him I really thought "That's how you live", because he seemed an absolute peasant in his response to life – it was so direct, two feet on the earth and solid. And yet underneath it was a tremendous shrewdness. He has a real gift for writing and you felt when he cooked, or when he wrote poems or when he drew, the same kind of animal conviction came into it. Even watching him smoke a cigarette had the same effect. You felt everything he did had this reality about it. People like that are the world's magicians. They have a kind of elemental magic about them – Picasso is another – they come from the centre of the earth somewhere and they just have it.'

JEAN ANOUILH

No playwright has bridged more successfully between the highbrow and middlebrow audience than Jean Anouilh. His plays may no longer have the same appeal to the intellectuals that they had in the late thirties and the forties but he is still popular. In 1971 he had three plays on in Paris simultaneously – two new plays, *Les Poissons rouges* and *Ne reveillez pas Madame*, and a revival at the Comédie Française of his *Becket*. Most of the twenty-seven plays he has written have been seen in all the major theatrical capitals of the world, and if we had statistics of how many performances various plays received in various countries, they would probably show that his have been more popular than the work of any other living playwright with any claim to seriousness.

Not that his popularity has been immune to changes of fashion. None of his plays were staged in Paris between 1962 *(Le Foire d'empoigne)* and 1969 *(Cher Antoine)* and he stopped writing for three years. 'Theatre captures me by its smell, and as those six years went by without any productions of my plays, I needed to rediscover theatre, to find the smell again. One day I was passing through Marseilles, and they were presenting a play in an old theatre, and I sniffed that strange smell, that bad old smell. I entered once again into the atmosphere of the theatre. It becomes a world where one doesn't think about what's going on outside – it's extraordinary, it simply doesn't count. Perhaps you notice that the weather's nice, that it's August. Any rehearsal is very much like any other but you enter into it completely, and the world outside no longer exists. I still remember that day. I told myself I must direct a play and I went back to Paris and I directed not one of my own plays but a play by Roger Vitrac, a friend of mine who died in 1952 without achieving any success.'

Anouilh went on directing plays by other writers in Paris and enjoying the freedom from the anxieties of having his own work presented to the critics. 'It's like sitting for an examination every single year. When you've done that all your life there comes a time when you just don't want to know whether you did well, whether you got eighteen marks out of twenty, or nought. I don't care any more.'

After a seven year gap in performances and a three year gap in writing he was naturally nervous about *Cher Antoine*, but it was an immediate success, and it is so closely in line with his earlier work that no one would have known about the discontinuity. As in so many of his plays, the focus is on life inside the theatre. But he always writes with his tongue in his cheek, and it is always dangerous to equate any of his characters with himself. 'People say they are stories in which my presence can be felt, especially the last two, but that's both true and untrue. You always put in something of yourself, but you borrow from other people, and you end up with something that isn't yourself, though everyone thinks it is. In Paris you have to have fun, and in *Cher Antoine* I amused myself a bit at the expense of the people who always say "That's him" by writing about a playwright. There are jokes for the initiated, like the line about this writer putting Germans into the play because he'd been in Germany. But most people didn't know that I had adapted Kleist's *Das Käthchen von Heilbronn*. But in spite of these jokes for the initiated, I write for the public.'

In his view, *Cher Antoine, Les Poissons rouges* and *Ne reveillez pas Madame*, which were all 'written in a sort of delight at having rediscovered the theatre', represent a slightly different kind of drama from that of his earlier plays, but he would like to go on to write plays in which the difference is more marked. 'I still have one more to write which is in line with the last three. Afterwards I want to do something else. Perhaps that's presumptuous, but you had George Bernard Shaw, who went on writing until he was ninety – right up to the end in fact. I've always thought there was an age when one had to stop. One has no more imagination, no more strength.

'What I need in order to write another kind of drama – if I'm not too old – is to be exiled, put in prison, something that would stop me from picturing the production. I don't write for an actor, I transcribe a performance that I visualize: I write a scene as I imagine it being played out in front of me. If for some reason destiny decreed that my plays were never again to be produced and that I was to write a different sort of play that I was never going to direct, I'd be able to write quite differently, benefiting from the freedom of not having to visualize it on the stage. I've been doing it so long that I can't help imagining the performance. And that's how I write it. It's like making a shorthand transcription of a play no-one else knows, with me as the only member of the audience. Paul Claudel, the old French playwright who wrote those mysterious and beautiful plays, was French Ambassador in Tokyo, and he was writing at a time when it was unthinkable that his plays would ever be presented in the fashionable boulevard theatre – which was dominated by writers like Henri Bernstein. So in that freedom he wrote plays that were absolutely mad, because he could imagine whatever he liked. Except for *L'Otage*, *L'Annonce faite a Marie* and *L'Echange*, they weren't staged until the forties. So he had his pockets full of plays. I've always said "I must save up for the future". I'd like to have five plays up my sleeve to be performed when I'm old. But when Claudel was seventy he had a new play produced in Paris every year. When I was a young man, a year never went by without a new production of a play by Claudel that had been in print since 1910. But my reserve stock consists of a single play. I must write some more. But that's what theatre is – to write for immediate production. After all, both Shakespeare and Molière did; they knew a play had to be finished within a fortnight – otherwise the theatre would have been empty. And that's a very good discipline for a playwright.'

People who remember the impact of Anouilh's early plays in the forties are likely to feel ambivalent about them, because the very qualities that made for the theatrical magic they generated depend on a distortion of reality which it is difficult to forgive. The purity and innocence of the young lovers was always contrasted simplistically with the gross, lip-smacking sensuality of their corrupt parents. Death was presented as the one attractive alternative to a life which seemed intolerable, not because the young heroes and heroines would be coarsened by the process of growing older but because they had no other refuge from the generation that was maliciously set on destroying their innocence in the process of finding fodder for its own coarse appetites. Plays like *Eurydice* (1941, known over here as *Point of Departure*) and *Antigone* (1943) now seem very strange to Anouilh himself. 'I get the impression I'm reading plays by my son – a young man who isn't me. There are certain things one still feels, because one's the same person, but those early plays seem awfully remote. I wrote plays which don't seem so far away, but everything I wrote in that early period, was very spiteful and derisive. I needed to sneer, to write sour comedy. Now I feel less like that. It was a sort of rejection of life by a young man who'd been a bit hurt by it. Death is the only thing that corrects the balance of things that have gone bad or erases the memory of them, but after a while you notice that death is just as absurd and just as dirty as life. It's equally ridiculous – not at all beautiful.

'But you must never confuse my own life with what I write, even though there is a secret zone or another creative life which is equally important, equally true, and this is perhaps one's real life. My plays are my only refuge. It's strange. I can't remember dates, I have no memory for things that happen to me. I'm the complete amnesiac. Everything that happens becomes remote. I remember nothing of my life before I was twelve. I'm completely asocial, and I forget social engagements, refuse to see people. But sometimes I meet someone – because I know everyone and everyone knows me – and when we say "Good morning. How are you?" I say to myself "This person is someone I detest, someone who's done something horrible to me" and I can't remember what! My plays are my only landmarks. For instance I remember the circumstances in which a play was written. I remember what happened at the time of writing *Antigone* or *Eurydice*. That's my calendar. It would be possible to write two parallel biographies of an author, one of the ordinary life he leads, the other of his secret life, of his creative sensitivity which also has a childhood, an adolescence and a maturity which bear no resemblance to his own childhood, adolescence and maturity.'

Disgust at life in his plays does not correspond to his own feelings about life. In his book *20th Century French Drama* (Columbia University Press) the American critic, David Grossvogel, suggests that Anouilh is like Montherlant in adumbrating a pattern in which the hero is called on to resume his virginity – that is, to give up establishing the illusion in this world either through the suicide of a return to his former being, or through the consecration of death in which the dream will endure. That is why so many end in a debauch of self-disfiguration during which words flow like blood from a gashed artery until the victim is dead. Only in death (that of non-believers) can the sham, the shame, and the world that made it, cease. Only in death will the illusion be reality. Here is truly Montherlant's "thirst for nothingness".

Anouilh's reaction to this was 'I don't think I've ever had this thirst for nothingness. Let's try to see things clearly: every young man of sixteen or seventeen thinks it would be better and simpler to die. But as soon as I came to grips with the weight of things, especially the weight of people, everything was different. I was a student for a year and a half and then I was a father – I've been a father all my life. I had beautiful children. And yet I wouldn't say this nihilism is insincere, or just a literary device. But equally I don't think it was a thirst for nothingness. There were times when I was tired of life, like everyone else, and thought it would be better to sleep. But that doesn't correspond to a thirst for nothingness in my own life. It's more like part of the creative life in which I had these feelings without knowing them in my terrestrial life. In any case I doubt whether I could have afforded those deep feelings. On the contrary, I had to build my life very seriously, defending it from other people. And there's something in that that doesn't go with the Nirvana thoughts of a man lying on a divan smoking cigarettes and thinking it would be better for him to die. I believe in a moral health which isn't in accord with that. But certainly, since it's in so many of my plays, it must have existed in my other life, the creative life. It was my first response to experience. These were the plays of a very young man and I remained a very young man for a very long time. I only began to understand things during the war or after the war, when I was thirty. As a young man I understood nothing. I couldn't have told you what a political party was. I knew nothing. I was just waiting for the Liberation. What was happening in France was terrible. We had to live through two years that corresponded to the Revolution of 1789 or 1792 and 93. At the age of thirty-four I didn't even know what the difference was between a Communist and a Socialist!'

Sometimes the connection between the two kinds of life can be closer than the artist himself realizes and it is possible that Anouilh's plays provided an outlet for emotions and attitudes which would otherwise have bulked larger in his relationships both with other people and with himself. It is odd though that poverty is such a recurring theme in his early plays – money being associated with corruption – when he had so little experience of what it felt like to be poor. He was the son of a tailor in Bordeaux. He went to Paris to study law and for a time he worked as Louis Jouvet's secretary. 'I was one of the first publicity agents in France; at the age of nineteen I was earning 3,000 francs a month, which is equivalent to 3,000 new francs today. I was twenty-two when my first play was produced. It was very successful but I didn't appreciate what was happening. Later on when I went through some bad years, I realized what luck I'd had to be so successful so young.

'After my first play I decided to give up public relations, and then I knew poverty, but it was only the poverty of making do with a coffee and a sandwich instead of a proper meal. It didn't harm me at all. It's through other people that one arrives at the knowledge necessary to write a character like Thérèse in *La Sauvage*, a play of mine which was massacred in London. But personally I've always felt rich, even when I had nothing. I never had a complex about poverty, although the money didn't start coming in till I was forty, forty-four. But I know what poverty is because I lived among poor people for a long time, and experienced it deeply through them, but the movement of revolt against it in the plays was never a personal one. In *Poor Bitos*, which was done in London with Donald Pleasence, people thought there was something of me in Bitos. That's not true at all. His political viewpoint is the opposite of mine. Even from the human point of view there's no correspondence. I detest men like that.'

In 1932 it was much more unusual than it is today for a playwright of twenty-two to have his work produced, but by then Anouilh had already been obsessed with the theatre for fourteen years. 'My theatrical life began when I was eight. It was the year of the Spanish 'flu epidemic and I caught it.

One evening on the esplanade at Royan, near the pier, there was a puppeteer with very large hand-puppets who was doing an artless production of *Romeo and Juliet*. I was taken ill during the performance. I had a temperature, I was shivering, I thought I was going to die. I was delirious for eight days, during which this production of *Romeo and Juliet* went on in my head, mixed up with feverish fantasies. And even now when I think of that play, I still picture those puppets and feel the emotions of that time.

'These childhood memories have enormous power. I'm sure that experience crystallized the mystery of the theatre for me, and it was the basis of my production of *Richard III*. We bought all the costumes from an old production of an opera called *The Huguenots* and we dressed everyone up in these old opera clothes. We infuriated Paris. Everyone said it was disgusting, revolting.'

Anouilh has exercised a powerful influence on the Paris theatre. His voice was one of the first to be raised in support of the original production of Beckett's *Waiting for Godot* (in Paris, January 1953) and in 1956 he turned Ionesco's *The Chairs* from a failure into a success. 'It was playing next door to my *Ornifle*, and the manager of the theatre said that no-one was coming to see it. So I wrote an article on *The Chairs* on the bottom right-hand side of the front page of *Le Figaro* and the next day the theatre was full. Things changed overnight. Now whenever a play does bad business I get asked to write on it. I have done it four or five times and it has always worked.

'I was very affected by that style of theatre, very interested, but it brought plenty of bad plays – pseudo-Becketts and pseudo-Ionescos. It provided a dangerous aesthetic for young people who don't have the genius of Beckett and Ionesco.' It was probably the imitation of Beckett and Ionesco that provoked Anouilh into writing a parody of that kind of play in *L'Hurluberlu (The Fighting Cock)*. 'One has the right to admire and then make a parody, to do something like that even if it is only to amuse oneself. It's not malicious.'

His first plays were directed by Pierre Fresnay. Then in 1937 *Le Voyageur sans bagages* was directed by Georges Pitoëff, whom Anouilh describes as 'the only theatrical genius I've ever known'. After directing *La Sauvage* in 1938, Pitoëff

died in 1939, and a long partnership began between Anouilh
and André Barsacq, who revived *Bal des voleurs* in 1940, going
on to direct *Le Rendez-vous de Senlis*, *Antigone*, *Roméo et
Jeannette*, *L'Invitation au Château*, *Colombe* and *Médée*. 'I left
Barsacq because whispering into someone's ear every five
minutes saying "It would be better to do it this way" is not
the same thing as to take charge and say "No, this is how it's
done", and explain directly to the actors. It's not possible for
me to direct my own plays abroad because I speak no foreign
languages. And then you get strange things happening because
the director can transform the whole feeling of the play. I've
had some splendid surprises. There was a play called *The
Waltz of the Toreadors* which was a complete flop in France.
I came to London to work with Peter Hall. I sat in the stalls
and got the impression that I understood English because I
recognized everything in the text. All the laughs came exactly
where I wanted them, and where I hadn't got them in Paris.'

Sometimes plays have done better when the production
departs from his original intentions. '*Les Poissons rouges* is a
play which I failed to direct as drily and cynically as I
intended, but one day we had the idea of staging it with two
comedians, two clowns. Since then it's had three hundred and
fifty performances and it's always sold out. So it works. It's
very funny. In Germany they produced it according to my
intentions, with villains, heroes and traitors. It didn't work.
It needs to be done with two comedians. The director changed
it into something serious – you see, a director can make or
break a play.'

Anouilh's methods of working have changed over the forty
years he's been writing for the theatre. 'In my early plays, I
tried to construct with great precision, knowing exactly where
I was going. But when you have everything worked out –
when you're hired to write the dialogue for a film which
already has a scenario – you need the qualities of a writer who
can construct secretly, apparently letting everything happen
by chance but actually foreseeing everything. It bores me if
I know where the plot is going exactly. But I think that when
I write a play, I don't have an exact subject that I could tell
anyone, but I have a character or two and, above all, an
atmosphere.

'I write quickly when something works. Either it fails com-

pletely or it goes very fast. I have the impression that it's a
play which already exists and which I saw a long time ago;
I try to remember it as if I had to tell the story to someone.
I feel as if I'd forgotten the details but that I'll rediscover
them in writing. I always feel I'm rediscovering something that
already exists.'

The development of a plot can be shaped by something
which happens quite by chance. He started working on *La
Répétition (The Rehearsal)*, which has a particularly involved
construction, when he was in the Midi, near Toulon. 'My
plays always start with a monologue because I don't know
what I'm going to do. I saw that woman, I had an idea of the
little governess, and of her husband, of a couple. The idea
came to me that they were wearing fancy dress, then I
thought they could be in costume because they were rehearsing a play. Then I began to write. Then it had to be a play
by Marivaux. I remember, I took my car and went to Toulon
to the bookshop and asked for plays by Marivaux and they
gave me Volume Two because they didn't have Volume
One. I went back to sit in the car and opened the book at *The
Double Inconstancy*. I remembered the play a little. I turned
over three pages, found a scene, and that's how I went on with
the play. It was quite by chance that I hit on *The Double Inconstancy*. If they'd given me Volume Three, I'd have written
a totally different play. I didn't know how it would develop
but I had that atmosphere of fashionable, hard-bitten people
with one of them suddenly experiencing a different kind of
love, purer. I had the feel of the play but not the details.

'Once I've written a draft, I hardly change it at all. I write
very little, only for two hours in the morning, and then I
stop even if it's going well – in fact especially if it's going
well, because that's when you write those beautiful scenes like
the ones in old plays, which go on and on. The next day I
bring someone else into the scene and it changes. Then I
type it in the afternoon, but I don't rewrite much. I'm lazy.
Perhaps if I did more revising it would be better.'

In fact, of course, as he knows very well, it would not. He
has perfected the technique of transcribing an imaginary performance to such an extent that he almost writes the
audience's reaction into the script, knowing exactly when the
laughs are going to come, and when the Parisian spectators

are going to applaud at the end of a long speech. Watching *Ne reveillez pas Madame* at the Comédie des Champs-Elysées, I had the feeling that it was the mood and the mixture of ingredients that the audience was responding to so enthusiastically, more than the story or the characters. The young girl was still just as innocent as the young girls in his early plays and the world of the theatre just as corrupt, but on this level the play is like a fairy story. The question hardly arises of whether the characters have counterparts in the world outside. Most of all Anouilh is fortunate in the way that he seems to be able to please himself and his public at the same time, with the same well-tried but still mellow blend of comedy and pathos, past and present, theatrical theatricality and theatrical reality, nostalgia and disillusionment, sentiment and satire. And if there are many who find the old magic no longer works, there are many who find it still does.

PETER BROOK

The art of the director is a comparatively young one. Until the middle of the nineteenth century, what happened on the stage was controlled mainly by the playwright or the leading actor, and much that is carefully regulated today was left to chance. The candle-lighting that was used until the eighteen-forties left a large part of the stage in semi-darkness and when gas lighting was introduced it was the prompter who directed it. Throughout the first half of the century rehearsals had nothing like the importance they have today. Rehearsal periods were brief and they were used merely to sketch out groupings and movements of the supporting company in relation to the leading actors – not to develop characterizations or mould a *mise-en-scène*.

In the eighteen-fifties, thanks to actor-managers like Charles Kean and the Bancrofts, and to writers like Dion Boucicault and W. S. Gilbert, progress was made towards organizing acting performances, theatrical effects and lighting into a more coherent shape, but the turning point for the London theatre did not come until 1881, when the Duke of Saxe-Meiningen brought his company to Drury Lane, seven years after it had made an equally crucial impact on the Berlin theatre, showing what could be achieved in production when a director combined the talents of artist, planner and disciplinarian. In 1890 Stanislavski watched the Duke's stage manager, Ludwig Chronegk, directing the company in a Moscow rehearsal. 'I started to imitate Chronegk,' he wrote, 'and with time I became a producer-autocrat myself, and many Russian directors began imitating me as I had imitated Chronegk.'

This then was the start of the autocratic tradition which was to survive, in England, into the middle of the present century, and, on the continent, is not dead even now. What it meant in practice was that the directors planned not only the

shape but the detail of his production before he had his first
rehearsal with the actors. Stanislavski has described how he
prepared *The Seagull*: 'I shut myself up in my study and
wrote a detailed *mise-en-scène* as I felt it and as I saw and
heard it with my inner eye and ear. At those moments I did
not care for the feelings of the actor! I sincerely believed it
was possible to tell people to live and feel as I liked them to;
I wrote down directions for everybody and those directions
had to be carried out. I put down everything in those production notes; how and where, in what way a part had to be
interpreted and the playwright's stage directions carried out,
what kind of inflections the actor had to use, how he had to
move about and act, and when and how he had to cross the
stage. I added all sorts of sketches for every *mise-en-scène* –
exits, entries, crossings from one place to another, and so on
and so forth. I described the scenery, costumes, make-up,
deportment, gaits, and habits of the characters, etc.'

Later he became less dictatorial, and in any case few
directors went into such meticulous preparatory detail, but
generally their method was to block all the moves in advance,
devoting the early rehearsals to telling the actors where to
come in, when to sit down, when to get up and look out of
the window. Later more detail would be imposed on them
within the outline that had then been determined.

Some directors, of course, were less autocratic than others.
Athene Seyler remembers working for Sir Gerald du Maurier,
who at one rehearsal said to her: 'Now darling, this is your
scene. Where do you want to sit and where do you want the
others?' This was not so much sharing the initiative with her
as handing it over to her.

It is only against this background that the importance of
Peter Brook's achievement can be understood. As he says
himself, 'Today you find it very hard to find a young director
who works anything out on paper. He realizes that things
evolve with a group. At first I was very much on my own in
this directing method. I was working against the tradition,
which was the tradition of the prompt book, of the director
arriving with a bulky book in which it's all worked out and
written down. And this was considered a sign of serious work.
I resisted it, believing that this was theoretical work, that any
work done by somebody before rehearsals is work done in

theory. It isn't living work. The living work is done on the spot, on the floor, with the actors. I, for this reason, like to develop everything through trial and error and experiment and improvisation with the actors.'

It was in his seventh professional production, and his first at Stratford-on-Avon, *Love's Labour's Lost* in 1946, that he discarded the old method of directing. He had prepared his production very carefully, working with a model of the set and cardboard figures to represent each character. He had written down all the moves he wanted. But on the first morning of rehearsals he found that instead of helping his relationships with the actors and their relationships with each other, his annotations were merely getting in the way. He found the courage to put his script aside, and since then he has never gone back to the old method of directing.

This does not mean that he now goes to the first rehearsal of a new production with no notion in his head of what he wants. But it is difficult for him to know how the ideas, the images and the inclinations that he starts with will be articulated in the work that is done with the actors in rehearsal. He explains it by analogy, pointing to the difference between a painter's or sculptor's methods of working and a composer's. 'Before he picks up his pen a composer has a complete and detailed image in his mind of a full symphony orchestra with each line in movement. He writes down the structure which has developed almost complete in his mind, and then many musicians don't change anything. And you contrast this with a sculptor who has in front of him a big block, whose intention is that he is going to search for a certain shape within that block. But stroke for stroke he is amending and changing that intention – otherwise it would never really emerge. The greatest example of this is in the Picasso film, showing Picasso reaching the end of his intention by endless apparent empiricism – one dot leading to a line, leading to a new thing erased . . . It's as though one starts from something that one feels very strongly. One can even talk about it and define it to a degree, but it hasn't quite got a form, and you go towards that with the people concerned – amending, changing, adapting, finding – and at the end, as the form emerges, you realize that this is where you've been going from the start.'

Naturally, for actors who had grown up under the old

directorial tradition, being effectively formed by it, it was not
easy to take advantage of the new freedom. 'It's only comparatively recently that a *whole* theatre, a whole new generation of actors to a man, accept a method which an older
generation – almost to a man – refused. I'd say that most of
the older actors I have directed, I found very difficult to work
with: whether it was that they were unsympathetic, or perhaps alien, I found it hard to find any particular taste or
enjoyment for their way of work. I worked as a necessary
evil with lots of actors who I knew were accepting a method
from me because it gave good results, but which they couldn't
understand and didn't like. And I was accepting from them a
sort of resistance, although I felt their approach to the work
was wrongly stolid.

'Today with any young actor that I know, any actor of
what I would call the new generation of English actors, this
doesn't arise, because this way of work corresponds to the
way they would work instinctively, even if nobody were there
telling them. And in that way people like Edith Evans – and
a hundred others – belong to a school in which the dream is
the director who walks in on the first day in a purely dictatorial and arbitrary way and says a hundred things they can
write down in the margin, which they will then take as gospel.
They won't have their opinion asked, won't contribute. They
will just take, and, having done that, they then expect to be
left alone, pretty well. They will obediently absorb those
things and then as long as they aren't changed, they've got
that bit out of the way, and they concentrate on developing
their work by repetition. This to me is a ghastly method, but
for a school of actor, for a type of play, the sort of play that
was current thirty years ago, it led to good results.'

The one actor of the old school with whom Brook found
an immediate and instinctive rapport was John Gielgud. 'With
us there had been a *very* deep one from the second we began
to talk to one another. I remember that one of the reasons
we liked working together was that both of us work very
empirically. Neither of us believes in starting from a set,
established plan.'

Temperamentally Gielgud is strongly disposed to a trial-
and-error approach. 'It's the way he always worked – he can't
think ahead, he can only work by trying, and as he has this

endless series of ideas, he immediately sees every possibility, and so invariably very comic things happen at rehearsal. He starts a sentence and says "I wonder if it wouldn't be a good idea if I came in from the left . . ." And before he has finished that, his mind has got tired of the idea and so, as he's explaining it to us, it's "Or maybe I should come in from the right?" And when on the first rehearsal I said to him "John, you come in from the back," before I'd finished that, he cut me up and said "Yes, but wouldn't it be better if I'm already discovered in a chair?" And before he'd finished that I saw the advantage of him being in a chair, but that gave me the idea that maybe even better than sitting in a chair, would be him lying on his back, and I say "You mean lying on your back?" And he said "Yes, marvellous, but then if I were lying on my back, I could be wheeled in on a stretcher". We found that we were both thinking in exactly the same way – often to the dismay of the cast who would find this endless change very disturbing. By the time one had said to some of the other actors "Now, you go there and you go there, we're going to try it out this way", either John or I had seen the disadvantages, and said "It's not worth trying that. It's no good anyway. Let's try something else".

'But on the whole, what it meant was that work would be experimental, high speed, and in the course of it John would improvise. In this sense he belongs completely to the most free and modern school. He wouldn't admit this all that readily, but he does everything by pure improvisation. So he improvises in one of many different keys of playing, explores something – says "Well, the character no doubt at this moment is ferocious", and as he begins to speak the line ferociously that gives him the idea that the character really may be meaning to say that line very gently, and he does it, tastes it, by doing it in a gentle way. In this way, over the course of two or three days, an enormous number of variations have already been explored; I then found the difference between John and myself was that John would tend to carry on endlessly with this process. In fact you know that famous story of him changing moves after the last performance of a play. Because his restlessness is permanent.

'Mine is different. With me it's like a golf ball – when you play as badly as I do, once a year, at the seaside on the putting green, where the ball always goes across the hole and never in, you go round and round and round the hole until eventually you get a right hit, and the ball goes in. That is where we differ – that I do use this method to winnow away the inessential and then suddenly recognize what we're looking for. With John it's at that point, towards the end of rehearsals that I've suddenly been able to dictate to him his own performance. In other words dictate to him his own discovery, not mine. People often ask directors: "Do you tell the actor what to do, do you tell an eminent actor what to do, or does he tell you?" And of course it never works that way, but with John it's the reverse of that. In the fourth week of rehearsal I'd say to John "John, you do this line in this way", and he's delighted to be reminded because it falls into place, and he suddenly remembers that *was* the best way and that *does* tie up with what I'm doing. And that's where there has been a perfect collaboration between us, because I've been able to help him to play the performance that he really set out to play, but which he could easily have blurred for himself with over-rich material.'

This goes a long way towards explaining why five of Gielgud's best performances have been the ones in which he was directed by Brook – Angelo in *Measure for Measure* (1950), Leontes in *The Winter's Tale* (1951), Jaffier in Otway's *Venice Preserv'd* (1953), Prospero in *The Tempest* (1957), and Oedipus in Seneca's *Oedipus*, adapted by Ted Hughes (1960). 'If you look at John in films, and if you look at John in his reading, *The Seven Ages of Man* which is one of the most remarkable things he's done, you see very clearly the difference between the very simple, very true and very realistic actor that there is contained in John, and John's extravagances or mannerisms, as they've been called at different times. The part of John that's a director is always concerned with the show as a whole, so when he directs himself he always neglects his own performance – he knows this – and consequently whenever he directs himself he always goes out on an enormous tour, recognizing that it's only in the tenth week of the tour that he begins to concentrate on getting truly and deeply inside his performance, and closing himself to a degree to what's going on around him, so that he can then concentrate on his work. Up till then he's improvising, and he's improvising off the top of his head, and so he uses devices, tricks, mannerisms – tricks really is the best word for it – he uses a series of tricks to get himself through the parts he hasn't yet deeply felt and resolved.

'A circumstance which is bad for John is when he is working with an unsympathetic director; another is when he is rightly cast and well directed but in a play that isn't right, that isn't going well. Then John's fantastic and highly developed sense of responsibility to an audience is greater than his responsibility to himself and so, of the two integrities, John, unlike a lot of other actors, will sacrifice not only himself but sacrifice the reality of his own work for the sake of not letting down the audience. So that again, where another actor would remorselessly plod forward developing his own role, even if the play is going badly and there are coughs out front, John, the moment he hears a cough, will sense that the house is restless and will produce some brilliant but well-tried stage trick to catch the audience's attention. That's where his great professionalism and his enormous experience are both a virtue and a vice, a manifestation of John's generous and open quality. And in that way it's a great virtue. It is also a vice because in all artistic work there comes a point where only selfishness can carry the artist through to the point he wants to reach. At that point John can easily lose his way.

'Another way in which a director can help John, is concentrating on him more than he would concentrate on himself, creating for John a climate of selfishness that he won't create by himself. So that to direct John you recognize that if you don't intervene till the last day of rehearsal, he will be interested in other people, their scenes, trying things fifty ways and so on. What you do is gradually build a glass wall around him, with an intense spotlight in the middle of it, so gradually, as rehearsals develop, you say "No John, that's none of your business, don't worry about the third act, leave that to the writer. Don't worry about the girl – she's getting on fine", until gradually his sights begin to turn in, despite himself, on his own work. It always has a shedding effect, as it has with all artists, because as their work develops they begin to shed the unimportant to get closer to the essential.'

Working on *Measure for Measure*, both Brook and Gielgud had certain preconceptions, but these were more a springboard than a straitjacket for the work done in rehearsal. Brook says that from the beginning he would have had 'a sense of Angelo, a lot of images, impressions, faces, facets of him, not yet in clear shape. And I'm therefore open to discover, although if someone were to ask me, I'd say "Of course he's in a wild temper here. That's my impression," and I'd be certain that when I start rehearsing this with someone else, that's going to be changed, so I'm not locked at all to that idea. And I then start doing that with John who, because he would have the same feeling, takes this line in which Angelo is clearly in a fury, and would suddenly try it not moving. Now, where another, a different kind of actor would make his suggestion in intellectual terms, and say "Look, I've been thinking of an idea and I think that many impulsive men in moments of great stress are motionless", with John it comes out of instinct in terms of behaviour at the moment, so he wouldn't know why, he would just say "Let's try doing the line motionless". He would just have that smell of something, and doing it motionless, suddenly a line that's apparently a loud, passionate and flamboyant line, will suddenly *isolate*, and at that second, if he is suddenly sensed rightly, you get a clue to Angelo. Suddenly Angelo appears for a moment, and because of that you see him as he could be twenty lines later, in a quite different light. So there, either you or John or both seize on it and say "Ah! But were that true, then we could start quite differently in the following scene". It's a form of impressionism. Once a true detail is found, it gives you a little more light, but the reason you pick that detail and not the other is because you do know ahead – otherwise you wouldn't recognize it. It's this thing of recognition. There is a pre-knowledge, based on study, on turning things over, on trying to define for yourself as much as you can, and John, like me, has that pre-knowledge, and will talk endlessly about it before starting rehearsal. Neither of us will say "Oh we can't talk because we don't know". We have strong theories about it which we'll lay down as law and say "Oh undoubtedly he's this, that and the other". Except that the next day, if anyone says "But you were saying yesterday . . ." we say "Oh, but that was yesterday". But at the time one believes it.'

*   *   *

It therefore seems slightly surprising that Brook should have so much liked Gielgud's 1950 *Lear*, which was founded on a 1940 production by Harley Granville-Barker, a director who knew exactly what he wanted before he went into rehearsal. 'That in fact was one of the most impressive experiences I've ever had in the theatre. I thought he was absolutely marvellous and although, years later, when I did *Lear*, I did it quite differently, I thought at that time if I'd done it with John, I would have been treating John in that particular experience the way John was treated by Granville-Barker. I would have followed him, because it seemed to me to have a ring of absolute truth and authority.'

Throughout the fifty years of his career, Gielgud has found no directors with whom he has been more in tune than Brook and Granville-Barker, who could hardly have been less alike in their methods of working. But this is Brook's explanation of the paradox: 'If Granville-Barker gave John everything from the start and said "The character is like this, that and the other" – because he was making suggestions which were in tune with John's general feeling – then I'm sure that on the first day with Granville-Barker, he gave himself over with the same relief as with me when I would do that same thing with him on the last day of rehearsal. And with John – it would be unthinkable with any other actor – on the last day of rehearsal very often I would start from the beginning of the play and say "Now John, that bit you remember where he is serious, and now it leads through the bridge of this to where he is not so serious and beginning to laugh" – and give him this pattern. I would do it on the last day, built out of what we had found together. But in fact, when the day came, he was only too pleased to find somebody he trusted telling him, in very clear terms, a series of things, every one of which he would then undertake to do because they made sense to him. Now because Granville-Barker was the only person whose general feeling and understanding of the play completely coincided with John's, then John could go towards him feeling that "Whatever this man says is what I would discover if I worked for three months on the play". That process happened on the first day, so when Granville-Barker said "As you come on in *Lear* you are this and that", John had no wish to argue . . . or simply, as I said earlier, one sets out towards something and when one

recognizes it, then the process of search is over. I think that
with Granville-Barker he recognized immediately that this was
right.

'All sorts of roads lead to Rome, and the method of the
director being right, the method of the director working
everything out ahead of time and then giving it to the actor,
is again a perfectly sound method if the director is absolutely
right. If I had the capacity, which is alien to my whole nature,
to sit at home and think out a play not only completely, which
anyone can do, but absolutely unerringly rightly, then there
is no reason why they shouldn't. But in fact what happens is
that the directors who use that as a method think wrongly and
then cling to what they have thought out, because otherwise
their authority is challenged, and that's why in most cases it's
a bad method. But if a man has the capacity that Granville-
Barker clearly had of thinking rightly, he presents simple out-
lines which the actor can then fill with his own flesh and blood.
Because an actor, if he is doing something that is given to him
that is right, always clothes it with himself.

'An author writes a role, a Shakespearean role in which
every word is rigorously laid down, but the completeness of
that structure doesn't take away from the actor's contribution.
On the contrary it sucks the actor's individuality into it and
that's the same with a director like Granville-Barker. He
would be working like the author.

'Today everything is different, all sorts of values being
different, ways of work different. In Granville-Barker's day,
it was a very much more stable society and therefore a more
stable world image. The Shakespearean world as he saw it, and
conceived it, in a completely coherent manner, was something
that could be given to an actor who shared so many of the
same world values as Granville-Barker, in a way that enabled
the actor to find it very close to himself.'

Of Brook's five productions with Gielgud, the most revolutionary and the remotest in style from anything Granville-
Barker might have done was unquestionably *Oedipus* at the
National Theatre. 'The only reason I did *Oedipus* was as a
real homage to John. I hadn't worked with him for a long
time. In fact I went to Vivien Leigh's memorial service and
John read the address, so marvellously and so movingly that
this was very much on my mind when out of the blue the

National Theatre asked me to do this *Oedipus*. Reading it I thought "Well, here is the field for a most interesting experiment. This is a play that on the one hand can only be done in terms of group work – that's the only way that the text and its choruses can be realized, and the only people to do this chorus are not chorus people but the very best and brightest and sharpest young actors with the willingness and openness to do the work necessary. And yet this is a play which depends on the word, which to a degree often defeats some of the most interesting actors, who have developed great possibilities of what they call corporal expression, great emotional freedom, but who are eventually at a disadvantage to John for instance when it comes to what he can do so marvellously in his reading." And I thought, here is an opportunity to make a living bridge through work between a whole range of actors. If we all worked together in a particular way, we could evolve a new style for this play that would depend in equal measure on the contributions brought by different schools and would be a product of the two. With that we started on this long series of exercises where the young actors' real appreciation of John was something quite different from what happens when a leading actor rehearses his part and a lot of young actors sit respectfully on the side. John threw himself into the group exercises on exactly the same level. It's equally difficult for everyone but not for one second did it occur to John that he had any special position or privilege. Artistically he was starting from zero and so were the others, and they would attempt the same exercises in the same way. He was always at a disadvantage because a young actor could do physical leaps and turns and twists in a way that obviously he couldn't.

'Then, as the exercises developed and got more advanced, there were things done with great difficulty with the voice and the gesture, and suddenly he would do something so marvellous that other actors who now knew him, not as the John Gielgud of books and photographs but as a man working with them, were acquiring a new admiration and an artistic respect for the fact that he was doing something which they realized was way beyond what they could have found, something that came from the depths of his talent and imagination. Out of that grew a very good relationship and out of *that*, an exchange of influence. And undoubtedly the total level of quality and attitude of speech of all the other actors was affected positively by the presence of John in the company, while John's use of his body and his attempting to use it and relate it to the part were also affected. Because for the first time, his interest and respect for what all the young actors are trying to do was caught in a new way, because he was working with them.'

This phrase 'build a living bridge' is characteristic of Brook and his whole way of working. The director, unlike the painter or the sculptor, is always working with living material, and the moment that matters is the moment of performance, the moment of living contact between actor and audience. This is why he distrusts abstractions, definitions, attempts to impose patterns from outside. At an early rehearsal of *A Midsummer Night's Dream*, an actor asked him 'How can you define what it is that we are looking for?' To questions like that his answer is always the same: that the work done in rehearsal, which goes in a thousand different directions, is always aimed at a definition, but if the definition could be formulated in advance, the work wouldn't be worth attempting.

He does not believe in following a straight line. 'I believe on the contrary that the only way one finds anything is through the radar system of finding one point, two points, three points, and somewhere in between those is what you are looking for. For this reason I've really spent all my working life in looking for opposites, from very early on. If I had worked in Shakespeare, I would then want to do a commercial comedy, if I'd done a commercial comedy I'd want to work in television, and if I'd worked in television I'd want to go to opera. And this to me is a dialectical principle of finding a reality through opposites. So that a line, in a way that can be pinpointed, is to me immediately suspect. So the moment someone suggests "I see, your line is towards ritual theatre" – another totally meaningless label that has been plonked onto a certain type of work – the moment I'm told my work's ritualistic, my instinct is to look for everything in it that is not ritual. And, when I'm told it's not ritualistic, then "ritual" begins to take on a meaning.'

One of his main reasons for wanting to tackle *A Midsummer Night's Dream* was that it constituted such a contrast with everything he had been doing since 1964. 'I find the material I've been working on has taken on a certain gloomy consistency. It's one of the reasons why it seems to me impossible to do even one more piece of work within that key. Because it seems that having worked on the *Marat-Sade*, *US*, *Oedipus*, and a series of *King Lears* spread over seven years, including years on the film version, it's absolutely essential to go to another part of the world where there is a different form of life enjoyed, as there is in *A Midsummer Night's Dream*. If one's only inside tragic material it's yet another false view of reality. Tragedy isn't total reality, it's a part, a version of reality, not a complete one, and one can't but feel in the end that something is lacking within it. When we did *US* we tried very hard to discover how it was possible to reconcile the horror of a living world situation such as Vietnam with a need to explore it and talk about it through a comic language. A tragic language seemed so woefully inadequate, though in fact the collaborators who worked on it, particularly Albert Hunt, have a very strong social sense and a sense of the relationship of farce to truth. At *US* we were continually moving into burlesque and farce as being perhaps the only way that one can deal with extreme horror. This was much misunderstood by many of the brilliant intellectuals who complained that it was unworthy of a serious theme not to have a certain intellectual seriousness in approach. But we very rapidly discarded that as being more unreal. The sort of academic and serious analysis of the meaning of Vietnam seemed to be farther from its reality than burlesque.'

In some ways each production that Brook has done represents a turning point in his development, but his experimental season at the LAMDA Theatre in 1964 was a particularly important one. With Charles Marowitz as his co-director he was working with a predominantly young group of actors from the Royal Shakespeare Company, devoting a great deal of time to developing a feeling of ensemble through improvisation and acting exercises. He was to go on to work with what remained basically the same group in a private production of Genet's *The Screens* (1964), then in Peter Weiss's *Marat-Sade* (1964) and in *US* (1966).

The title for the LAMDA season – 'Theatre of Cruelty' –
was much misunderstood. 'Although the work itself was presented with a quotation from Artaud* which established absolutely precisely his extraordinary definition of cruelty as being
a form of self-discipline, and therefore cruelty meant cruelty
to oneself. That notwithstanding, for years and years after
that, question after question would be put to one towards
an apparently avowed taste for sadistic material, sadistic relationships with an audience, with actors and so on and so
forth.'

Artaud's hostility to the theatre of words and personal relationships, his interest in ritual, myth and magic, gave Brook
a number of valuable cues for a series of experiments both in
actor-audience and actor-actor relationships. By working intensively with a young group, especially in non-verbal improvisations, Brook found it was possible to create very strong
bonds between members of the ensemble. This was not
altogether a new discovery, though. Already in 1960, working
on the Paris production of Genet's *The Balcony*, he found
that 'Long evenings of very obscene brothel improvisations
served only one purpose, they enabled this hybrid group of
people to come together and begin to find a way of responding directly to each other'. But certainly it was useful in 1964-
66, to do four successive productions with the same group.
Then in 1968, with *Oedipus*, he cut free and used none of the
actors he had used before.

The 'Theatre of Cruelty' season was also a turning point in
that it taught him the value of working with actors over a
longish period without having to produce a polished production as an end-result of the work. An invitation from Jean-
Louis Barrault gave him a chance to create an international
centre of research for actors from different countries under
the auspices of the Theatre des Nations in Paris. The experiment was interrupted by the student rebellion, but in July
1968, at the Roundhouse in London, the group presented a

---

*In *The Theatre and Its Double* (1933) Artaud wrote 'Our long habit of
seeking diversion has made us forget the idea of a serious theatre, which,
overturning all our preconceptions, inspires us with the fiery magnetism
of its images, and acts upon us like a spiritual therapeutic, whose touch
can never be forgotten.

'Everything that acts is a cruelty. It is upon this idea of extreme action,
pushed beyond all limits, that theatre must be rebuilt.'

series of exercises based on *The Tempest*. The actors had reached a stage in their work where they needed the sounding-board that only a live audience could provide, but it was made clear to the public that what it was watching was a workshop. 'We had no sense of obligation to deliver *The Tempest*. Consequently we were free, we could do a *Tempest* in which nine-tenths of the text was inaudible, incomprehensible. This didn't worry us. People who reproached us with that were making a useless reproach. It would have meant many months of work before we could have recovered that same freedom and yet made every word and every line live completely. To do neither thing would have been a horrid half-way house where we would have had to become much stiffer and conventional to deliver the text, or we would have had to say "To hell with the text. This is ruining our newly found freedom. Let's not endanger our freedom. Let the text look after itself." Both of which would have been rotten solutions if the aim had been to present Shakespeare's play. The only good solution would have been to have gone on working month after month to the point where, in presenting the text, we could have found all the freedom there was in the exercises.'

One of the exercises was what Brook calls the mirror exercise. Two actors face each other, one trying to copy every movement the other does as if he were his mirror. This is 'an exercise by which two actors begin to work in harmony. Then four, then six and then eight, and then twelve, until the whole group is working in harmony. This is a basis of working, the product of an actual series of exercises of many different sorts by which the group works very freely together. And this is something that always has to be renewed. The fact that a group worked well last week doesn't mean that it happens this week. It always has to be re-exercised. New problems arise, so that a play can't be approached unless the group is in a good state of preparation.' This particular exercise was not used in the preparation of *A Midsummer Night's Dream*, but, as Brook put it, '*The Tempest* exercises in one way were everything we're doing in the *Dream* or directly related to the *Dream*, which is a pure extension of that work'.

Just as in *Oedipus* Brook had been handicapped by an old-fashioned theatre (the Old Vic) so, in the *Dream* it was a big disadvantage to be preparing the production for the theatre in Stratford-on-Avon. But if Edward Gordon Craig did little work in the theatre because prevailing conditions fell so far short of his ideals, Brook is essentially a realist. 'I have never despised or tried to reject the existing theatre, because it is what it is. Some of it is very poor, and some of it is very good, and some is a mixture of the two, but it exists. And as long as it exists, it is a requirement that has to be fulfilled. Now Stratford and part of the Administration exist in dramatic forms that are criticized very strongly within the directorate. It exists for instance in buildings that I dislike. I think the Aldwych is an awful theatre, and this Stratford theatre, which changed its name to the Royal Shakespeare Theatre, but still remains the Stratford Memorial Theatre, built by a lady who knew nothing about theatres and approved by a committee of local worthies who knew nothing about theatre, has been amended and amended by a series of directors over the years, but it still is not the theatre that is needed for playing Shakespeare. The acoustics are really poor and Shakespeare of all things demands sensitive speech. The first requirement of a Shakespeare theatre is an acoustic miracle in which actors can play freely and lightly in a warm living way, so that the colours that they bring to the words are very rich. If you have to play Shakespeare in a cruel theatre, where, if you don't face front and speak at a certain pitch, at many points you can't be heard, then you're in an instrument which, by its very nature, introduces tension into playing and precludes a great number of qualities that a much more relaxed playing produces.

Now Peter Hall has tried to change this situation by using enormous initiative in getting the Barbican; 'one day we may hope that someone will set fire for a second time to the Stratford-on-Avon theatre and it'll be rebuilt.* It is inadequate and can't fulfil the needs of a group trying to present Shakespeare because it doesn't correspond with what any of my colleagues really needs. But it exists. It would be woefully inadequate and irresponsible to say "So we abandon it." We have to do as best we can with what are still the best conditions that exist in the world at this moment for putting on Shakespeare – which are the possibilities given by this imperfect but evolving organism called the Royal Shakespeare Company.

*The original theatre, built in 1879, was destroyed by fire in 1926. The new theatre, designed by Elizabeth Scott, was completed in 1932.

'*A Midsummer Night's Dream* has to happen within the context of this theatre. Now that means that I cannot think of *A Midsummer Night's Dream* within the context of the Roundhouse. While on the other hand my own work and the experiments which have been evolved are such that I cannot for one second believe that the type of proscenium theatre we work in with a thousand people sitting in fixed rows staring at the stage is in any way right for a modern audience.

'I feel this is completely out of date, not only as a fashion but out of date since it isn't a living relationship that really would make the most vital acts of theatre happen. I tried to do this in *Oedipus*, and *Oedipus* was an experiment which took us about as far as we could go in struggling against a given requirement, which was the architecture of the Old Vic Theatre. We tried to turn that into a virtue by encircling the audience with actors strapped to pillars. The sort of thing which would have been very natural at the Roundhouse was here a fight to the death against the building. In Stratford, to build platforms all over the auditorium, consequently cutting the one thousand seats down to five hundred would make it neither fish nor fowl. It would not be the Roundhouse, it's not the sort of work we could do in many other places. So the whole way of thinking has to be in a sense amended. But not the aim, because there's only one aim in any theatre work, and that is to reach a living event, a living experience; it is the means that have to alter. To make a living experience in one architecture demands quite different means from another.

'But it's like the difference between one play and the other. The moment you change plays or you change subject, all means anyway have to change. To me the continuity is always the same – trying to discover how a living event is made. You can make a living event by improvisations, without any material and a living event with existing materials may be quite different and in many cases more intense. When you deal with Shakespeare, the intensity of the material gives you the possibility of reaching an infinitely higher level of vitality in the event than could be achieved without that marvellous material.

'It's always the same problem – unimportant whether it's comedy or tragedy – how can you close the triangle between subject matter, the performers and audience? It's always the same task – three points that have to be linked. And always the problem's reopened because given conditions are always totally different. In this case the given conditions mean that a lot of what we did in the Roundhouse cannot possibly be applied directly, stuck on that stage. And yet other things can be applied very intensively but apparently indirectly.'

Rehearsing the *Dream*, Brook started with a lot of exercises. In the way he now works, this always comes first. Second comes the understanding of the play – not an intellectual understanding but a translation of the printed text into living terms. 'When you have a play which is poetic and subtle to a degree, you can't achieve collective understanding – everybody understanding what they're playing – by the director making a speech, as a sort of pedagogue who has worked out what he thinks the play's about and then explains it to his actors. Eventually the quality of the result depends on a shared understanding, not on one man's view. For an actor to go on a stage with conviction, conviction that really carries to an audience, he has to know what he is talking about, and to know what he is talking about, he has to believe, and to believe means that he has to be inwardly committed. If an actor is given a point of view which he finds plausible but which he doesn't deeply feel, he may try his best to commit himself to it but it would be very different from the commitment of an actor who has really shared in the discovery. The actor who is trying to sell to an audience an idea or an emotion that he really isn't sold on himself feels shifty. But an actor who's representing something that he knows and has experienced and can defend as his own truth, has no embarrassment about presenting it. Quite on the contrary, he wishes this to be known.

'This is an enormous long way to go when you start with any subject. In the case of *US*, on the first day we gathered our actors together and said "Now what does everyone believe about the war in Vietnam?" And thirty opposing views arose, most of which were very vague, ill-informed and unformed. Three months later there was still a diversity, but the subject had been lived with, and the people who took one side or another took it with passionate conviction, because they had learnt their way into the subject. And when we had open debates afterwards, the actors each spoke very individually about what they felt.

'And in the same way, you start with the *Dream*. It's far from Vietnam, but a play with the greatest subtlety and mystery. But before a director and a group can find any forms by which this can be presented to the public, we have to explore, we have to learn for ourselves by first-hand experience what this play is about. Where somebody studying *The Tempest* in a library uses intellectual and analytical methods to try to discover what it is about, actors try to discover through the voice, through the body, through passion, through involvement, through experiment in action. And in that way, by trial and error and elaboration and rejection, the themes of the play become clear as they come to light, become visible. So the process of rehearsing a play like the *Dream* is very simple. You can read the play together two or three times and then it becomes boring. Soon you feel that first-hand experience is needed. In the case of the *Marat-Sade*, the first-hand experience we needed being about madness, for days we could use the true living material of each of the actors, who almost all had had an encounter with madness. The madness was either in his family, amongst his friends or in himself. So for days we could put aside the text and pour out together experience that related to it. Whereas with the *Dream* people don't come with the same amount of material on spirit life that they have on madness. According to statistics, three-quarters of the families in the world have madness in them, so it's instantly available. But you can't do a play about the spirit kingdom if the actors think it's just a lot of old shit. Well, you get a group of people and say "What do fairies mean to you?" No good answers will come out of that. And until you get past that stage you can't start working on *A Midsummer Night's Dream*. How can you get past it? Experience from everybody's life? "Has anybody here seen a madman?" Everyone says "Yes", "I know one", "I am one." "Anyone seen a fairy?" "No." "Are you a fairy?" Blushes, confusion. Right, one voice saying "Well, maybe". The only first-hand experience you can then get is trying to explore the text and that means using all the specific acting methods of which the work done in public on the Roundhouse *Tempest* was a partial reflection. That is the sort of thing which, when done by actors, and then examined and discussed by them all together, brings the play out in the open.

'For instance you can achieve exact relationships. In the case of *The Tempest*, the Japanese actor – by approaching Ariel through his breathing and through his body – made Ariel something very understandable. A certain force became completely tangible in something which to the Japanese would be easy to understand because it was the basis of the Noh theatre from which he came; he brought a certain type of sound, a certain type of cry, a certain type of breath. The idea of a force was truly represented, and so it could be discussed, it had suddenly happened – there it was amongst us. It was no longer "force", an abstract word, it was a reality, something that could influence another person. Now in the same way improvisations, amongst other things, can through a long process of time, begin to give one starting points from which to uncover the many worlds of the *Dream*, the interweaving levels of reality, the reality of Bottom, his world . . . What is this reality? What reality is it contrasted to in others? What reality is this contrasted to in the fairies? These vague and theoretical terms gradually become precise and clear to everybody, because everybody has gone through the same explorations together. But when, after a sufficient series of practical experiences, you come back to discussion and find the terms of reference have become stronger and clearer through work done, work shared, you begin to have a conviction which is your starting point. Through this come, right at the end of the line, the physical means and the imagery.

'In the case of a Shakespearean play, it is difficult to bring that freely discovered raw material into perfect harmony with a text that is absolutely set and can't be changed in any way. At this point there's always a nightmare period, because the discipline of a text is very hard to swallow. The moment the actor tries to concentrate totally on the requirements of the text, a lot of his freedom disappears. It's not his fault. It's completely out of his control. He respects the text and wishes to master it, but as long as the difficulties aren't completely overcome, one is corseted, imprisoned within the requirements which are always fantastically difficult in Shakespeare. Shakespeare has the same terrible difficulty that Mozart holds for

singers: there is no mercy, no indulgence, it has to be totally
mastered. There is a long period when the efforts to master the
discipline involve a total lack of that very freedom which gives
the life and the richness to any performance. No, either one
comes through this stage or one doesn't.

'Very early on in rehearsal, the actors did a free improvisation on *A Midsummer Night's Dream* and I think of all the
many years I've been connected with improvisations this was
far the most thrilling piece of joyous lunatic surrealistic free
theatre I've ever known. It was a performance for just those
of us who were there in rehearsal, completely off the cuff and
from which energy burst out and made something quite
memorable, a fantastic piece of collective invention. Everything
that was in the rehearsal hall was somehow pressed into service
and there was something like . . . the end of the *Marat-Sade*
when the whole asylum went berserk and wrecked the place.
When we made the film, this scene was so genuine that it
lasted three hours and the actors wrecked and set fire to the
set at Pinewood, and we filmed it over the three hours. It was
a great happening and there was this joyous release after playing that constricting, cramping film, to feel it was the end.
And everything really went mad. In exactly the same way
there was an explosion of energy in the *Dream* cast that
expressed itself in the most staggering invention. At the end
of it one had been present at a real theatrical event, an event
in the sense that it could never have been repeated. What we
had gained from our work was a marvellous feeling of excitement amongst everyone who had participated in it, and a
number of lights thrown on many parts of the play, just by
pure inspiration of the moment. But the moment all the energy
went on to working the text naturally, there was no longer
any energy left for this sort of spontaneous life, and so we had
to go into a stiff and rigid period.'

As in the work on the 'Theatre of Cruelty' and on *The
Tempest*, a point came where a sounding-board was needed.
'The rehearsal process is something that in theory is all private
until the first night. In fact the ebb and flow is more complex,
and there comes a point when the existence of an audience,
if the audience isn't destructive, crystallizes certain things,
reveals certain things – in other words presents a challenge and
a searchlight which enables you to take the work a good step

farther. Now half way through the rehearsals, already some-thing incestuous has come into being for the cast. The cast is too at home and in tune with itself, and its locked doors and closed walls. If there is an outsider there, already something for better or for worse emerges. That's why I've always felt that it's not possible to do experimental work without going out on a limb and exposing it, when we know that we are not ready. That's why for instance at LAMDA, nobody at the time could follow why we did a lot of exercises whose mean-ings at the time was considered incomprehensible. Only when people saw the *Marat-Sade* two years later did they see the relationship between them. But for us it was vital. It would have been masturbatory to have worked and worked and never taken the challenge of exposure and confrontation that there is, because then you realize where you're on a totally wrong track, where something is a genuine disaster, and you can bluff yourself for years if you don't face that awful moment of seeing that it's no good at all.

'Now in the same way in our work here, in the middle of rehearsals and three-quarters of the way through, one needs that confrontation. At the same time one is dealing with the most sensitive thing there is, which is human material, and everybody from actors to director is at this point very raw and very vulnerable and very susceptible, and one can be destroyed by a harsh and negative judgment. So that to show our work to critical adults could be purely destructive. That's why we were saying that the perfect audience for our purpose is an audience that has great attention and that has no judg-ments in the adult sense of the word, has a direct interest judgment, but not the sort of adult judgment that is really withering and paralysing for a sensitive actor. It's got to be quite different, it's not to be critical in that dangerous sense of the word. And at the same time, children are a generous audience and a very, very demanding audience. So you can't do bad work for children, you have to do work at your best. Probably they were the audience we needed.'

In most productions of the *Dream*, the fairies, the nobility and the artisans seem to constitute three separate worlds but, as Brook saw the play, they were 'three very intertwined and overlapping worlds. It's a play about worlds within worlds; it's not for nothing that it's a play about a play about a play.

Because one sees that these hard and fast divisions are just first level definitions and that the more you get into it, the more they evaporate and melt. For instance the same actor is playing Theseus and Oberon, the same actress is playing Hippolyta and Titania, and the same actor is playing Puck and Philostrate.'

He was also conscious of Shakespeare's very deliberate use of alternation between verse and prose. 'Bottom and the mechanicals speak in prose and it seems to me a clear starting point that the mechanicals are in a prose world which in Shakespeare always suggests that one has to look outward. The verse world is a world in which one must look inwards into the text, in the sense that it's a concentration of the meaning and that one can't start by a feeling that one has to embroider. Through the verse one must look into the intention: the moment that Shakespeare is writing in prose, it's almost as though there's an obligation to develop, as you would for instance a modern realistic play.

'The prose passages demand that turning into flesh and blood existence for which realistic elements have to be found and in *A Midsummer Night's Dream* the prose portions suggest a social context. The working men are putting on a play, which, if you carry it through quite simply, compels you to reconsider from scratch the place of Pyramus and Thisby. If you once imagine in terms of social reality a group of artisans attempting – because they believe in it passionately – to put on a romantic play, it seems obvious to think that the comedy should lie in laughing at unqualified people doing something badly. Are the mistakes of illiterate people funny, or is this a rather unpleasant upper-class tradition? And in fact I wouldn't even call it upper-class – a sort of middle-class tradition. Because the upper-classes and aristocracy have always had a much more generous attitude, like the Duke himself, who says very clearly in one of the most eloquent speeches of the play that when he sees a man stammering and shivering and blushing in front of him, he perceives his intention and doesn't find anything to laugh at in his mistakes and embarrassment and sweating palms. And here Shakespeare gives one of his major speeches to expressing a theme which cannot but throw light on a major portion of a play, which I think too easily is considered funny without the nature of that fun being really evaluated. Because if one once starts from a fellow feeling for the hard attempts of non-intellectual people to break into an imaginative world with love and respect and devotion, with their own untutored efforts, the play of Pyramus and Thisby at once takes off in a different direction. This is not interpretation but a direction dictated by a realism, which is called for by a prose world. And in the same way that the Stanislavski question of "What is Oberon doing in the wings?" is silly, the Stanislavski question of "What is Bottom or what is Snug doing?" is as pertinent as it is in Chekhov. And that is why in Shakespeare I have always maintained that there is not one style, there is not one method. That the glory of Shakespeare is the co-existence of a thousand opposites which in practical terms demand a thousand opposed and contradictory approaches to co-exist within one performance.

'I keep on saying to the cast – nothing is by accident in Shakespeare. Nothing can be explained away as the conventions of the time or "Oh well he did it because he didn't know what to do, or he wasn't thinking that . . ." If you come rigorously back to this, everything becomes a very difficult question to answer. "Why did Shakespeare, writing in the full flood of his talent, put Pyramus and Thisby in the key position?" The play could end without this last act, entirely. The whole of the story wraps up when dawn comes and the lovers are reconciled, and were it a Mozart opera, there you'd have your final sextet and go home. And he writes a last act that is apparently in dramatic narrative or neat comedy terms, totally superfluous.

'You can say one of two things. You can either take a camp and fruitless view which is to say "Well he wrapped his plot up by the end of Act Four and sat down to think what the hell am I going to do? And reached for a new idea". Or you can say he is a conscious writer, who knows what he's doing, when he puts the play-within-the-play in the star position at the end of the end and makes a whole act round it – an act that begins with a long and apparently gratuitous speech about the poet and about imagination – again not necessary. This is such a strong intention of Shakespeare's that one has to revise one's views of the entire play, asking what necessitates this and no other form of the last act. And why is it that the play in fact couldn't exist, couldn't have its meaning without this?

And the moment you open that question, once again the relation of Pyramus and Thisby to the Duke and lovers changes.

'The first production I did in this theatre was *Love's Labour's Lost*, and I did it by just the same premiss of saying nothing can be by accident. Therefore what can it mean – the entrance of Mercado at the end of the play? After a two and a half hour pastoral lyrical comedy without a single dark thought in it, suddenly death enters in the last reel. This seemed so fantastic an event that one couldn't not take it as a major intention. And I'd seen the play performed, I think, once upon a time, and had been amazed to see that this – as it had no place in comedy – was treated rather lightly, so as not to intrude too much. It seemed on the contrary that it was there as an intrusion, and we played it and rehearsed it and explored it as an event, a world-shattering event. And in fact, having done so, it amended one's feeling about the balance of the whole play. The taste of the play was totally changed by this artificial world having put up against it something very different – this reality intruding at the last moment. Even if it was an early play, it was not there for nothing. The whole play found its proper resonance in this dark moment at the end.

'It's the same process of thought that makes one say "If this is so clearly intentional, then all the lines, the curious jokes of the Duke, the odd difficult lines that come through the lovers' interventions – all need to be appraised very carefully". In *Love's Labour's Lost* the entrance of death at the end doesn't change your interpretation of anything that preceeds it, because it is a gratuitous act right out of the blue, like the killing of Cordelia in *Lear* suddenly as a thunderbolt that falls donk onto the play. It's not made inevitable by things that happen earlier. It's a twist.

'In *A Midsummer Night's Dream* when Hippolyta says "This is the silliest stuff that ever I heard", the Duke makes this marvellous statement about the whole pretentions of theatre. From our point of view, the difference between rotten acting and superb acting seems to be enormous. It's the bottom and top of the mountain. From a different point of view it's not all that important. What is important is not only what the actor is doing or what level the actor achieves, but what the spectator brings; the actor is searching for meaning that is only completed with the full, active co-operation and complicity of the spectator. Theseus says that depending on what we bring to it, the quality of what the mechanicals do can be made or marred, and that if our imagination enters in the right way into their efforts, they may pass for excellent men. Many things are said through this last scene which makes what we are speaking of much easier to define – clumsy people doing a bad play badly, noble people being poetic and brilliant, spirits being not as easy as all that; it is much more complex and in another way much simpler. Because they must say how that line echoes back to a line that again is not there for nothing. Not that Shakespeare didn't drop pearls of wisdom from time to time when he felt inclined, but in the middle of a farcically comic scene, when the mechanicals are rehearsing, they go through the whole history of the theatre, of what illusion is. The whole of Brecht's life's work is contained in the argument of whether you represent something by *being* it or by a token, like a man saying he's a wall. And at a certain moment, talking about the Lion, Bottom advises how to make a lion in a Brechtian sense, so that he presents Lion without there being any element of excessive emotion or involvement of the audience. Not only should he clearly say "I'm not the Lion but Snug the Joiner", but he adds this further line "Because I am a man as other men are". Now, if you relate that line which sings out of the text (although it's not meant to be a line suddenly delivered like "Oh what a piece of work is man") to the Duke's: "If we think no worse of them than they of themselves, they shall pass for excellent men", and you tie that to twenty other lines in different portions of the play, then a whole new scale of meaning begins to come out into the light.'

Any attempt to describe Brook's way of working, whether in his own words or not, is inevitably incomplete. Any description of what he gets actors to do with their bodies and their voices can be only partially successful. In *Oedipus*, for instance he worked for three weeks with the whole cast before showing any of them a script, and even if someone had kept a detailed log-book of rehearsals, it could tell only part of the truth about the exercises and experiments, about the strenuous physical and and psychological gymnastics or about the efforts he made to teach the actors to resonate from their chests after playing them records of Tibetan monks.

But this summing up would be more incomplete than necessary if I ended it without trying to give some impression of what the experience of working with him is like from the actor's point of view, and what effect it can have on an actor's development. Invariably, like psycho-analysis, the process is painful. And it goes without saying that there are some actors who maintain that the pain is unnecessary, that equally good results can be achieved without making them suffer. Others have found that they have gained insights into areas of their own reality which no other director could have given them.

The English actor, more than the Russian, the American, the Italian, the Japanese, generally feels inhibited about displaying raw emotion. One of the main virtues of English acting is its restraint, its coolness, its freedom from demonstrative self-indulgence, but one of the major disadvantages of that restraint is the filtering effect it has on the discharge of libidinal force, which often needs to be present during the creation of a characterization, even if it is only present in performance as a foundation, invisible to the audience. Without being entirely neutralized or entirely censored, these libidinal elements are sometimes tamed more than they ought to be, not by the director, but by the actor himself, though with the director's unspoken – perhaps unconsidered – acquiescence.

One actor who was talking to me about Brook used the word 'cruel', but immediately added 'I think he has to be. That's the way he has to work. I mean he doesn't leave you any options. You either resist and you get nothing out of it, or you lay yourself open, and have some fairly punishing rehearsals. I don't mean he's saying awful things or putting you down, but you feel that he's metaphorically trying to tear you, really tear something down there.'

Nearly all actors feel that there is a more savage side to their natures than usually gets shown in performance. They may be aware, when they sit in an audience and watch a great actor like Olivier, that part of his magnetism and of the excitement he generates depends on the feeling he gives of animal power which could be unleashed at any moment. But being aware of this is very different from being able to throw off the inhibitions that usually hold these dangerous-seeming forces in check. English acting is less restricted today than it ʾwas twenty years ago by the middle-class tradition of gentility and good manners, but most actors have an inherent resistance to displaying facets of their own personality which might strike an audience as unlikable. And beyond this understandable anxiety there are barriers that can be broken down only with the help of a good director. Probably none of our directors has been of more help to actors in this way than Peter Brook.

To take just one example, Ronald Pickup, who gave an excellent performance as the messenger in *Oedipus* who has to describe how the King blinded himself, told me how much Brook had helped him by telling him to rehearse the speech as if he were a gargoyle, a kind of monster. 'Just envisage yourself as a strange shape off a Gothic cathedral or a monster out of a voodoo ceremony, or something like that.' Pickup then rehearsed the speech in a much more grotesque way than it could be played in public. 'I was using the text, but he said "Feel free about warping words". The word *stand* didn't have to sound like *stand*. One could do anything with any of the series of words, but one was really concentrating on sound from back beyond the time words were invented. Just having the words vaguely sitting on top of it. I remember that exercise most vividly because I think that was the time when I felt it really broke through. And the most ugly, awful – but for that speech real and right – sounds were coming out. And then, as time went on, it was possible to integrate them. I also went through a period when I used to do it very statically, right from the beginning. And then it started to go a bit dead. And only some two or three days before we opened, he said "Forget all that business about coming forward and just doing it there. Do it in slow-motion, glazed time, as if you'd been stunned by what you've seen. Or if you want a naturalistic image, think of it being like a watchman, ringing a bell, announcing the news, going along the streets, telling it to the waiting population." So out of that came the thing of sludging through blood. Which also gave it more weight – because I'm a very lightweight actor. It made me feel more weighty than I'd ever felt before – heavier, in a good way.'

Peter Brook can even influence actors who have never worked with him. John Wood, who did not join the Royal Shakespeare Company until the *Dream* was in the repertoire found that it altered his whole conception of how an actor should be working. 'It's something to do with reaching back and down into the pre-history of which the language spoken on the stage is the Modern Times. You sat in the audience at the *Dream* and if enough of the actors and the audience were in the right frame of mind, the sensation was of being one of a circle of people where the actor-audience relationship as it usually is disappeared. One seemed to be part of a circle of people celebrating something or observing some ceremony. Religious words are perhaps the right words to use. It seemed to me that we all experienced and celebrated the terrible dark agonizing contradictions and horrors that forced Shakespeare to write *A Midsummer Night's Dream*. What we seemed to see was the lowest and farthest tentacles of the roots of a tree of which the foliage is the words.

'It was to me an extraordinarily opening experience. I admired very greatly what the actors were doing, the dazzling displays of skill which were then immediately revealed as mere skill, and denied. I think somehow we should all be doing that now. I think that actors should look at themselves in relation to the character that they are to play, not in the terms in which that entity is different from other people but in the terms in which it's the same as other people.'

PAUL SCOFIELD

The actor Peter Brook has used more than any other is Paul
Scofield, who has been in eleven of his productions. At
Birmingham Rep in 1945, Barry Jackson bravely entrusted the
twenty-year-old director with *Man and Superman*, followed
(after it had turned out successfully) by *King John* and *The
Lady from the Sea*, and in these three productions, Scofield,
who was then twenty-three, played John Tanner, the Bastard
and Dr Wangel. In Brook's 1946 *Love's Labour's Lost* at
Stratford-on-Avon he was the fantastical Spaniard, Don
Adriano de Armado, and in the following season's *Romeo and
Juliet* Brook cast him as Mercutio. In *Ring Round the Moon*
in 1950 he played both twins and in *Venice Preserv'd* (1953)
he was Pierre to Gielgud's Jaffier. Then in his season with
Brook at the Phoenix in 1955-6 he played Hamlet, the Priest
in *The Power and the Glory* and Harry in Eliot's *The Family
Reunion*. He was also Brook's Lear, starting in 1962 and
returning to the characterization in the film seven years later.

Like Gielgud, he finds that being directed by Brook is quite
a different experience from working with anyone else. 'Yes,
I think that whenever I work with Peter I find myself, as you
say, in a completely different category. But I have worked
more for Peter than I have for anybody else and we worked
together so very much at the beginning of our careers, that
it's probably less true of me than it is of John Gielgud. Because
I think Peter's influence is perhaps more alien to John – by
which I don't mean that I have resisted it in any way – than it
is to me. I grew up with Peter, and John was very much in a
strong and developed area of his own before Peter ever
entered it, whereas I was completely raw material when I first
worked with him. But I think that while I do, as it were,
switch on to a different wavelength with Peter, it's only because of my long association with him. I work in exactly the

same way with him as I do with anyone else. I don't change my responses, although I feel much more at home with him.'

The extent to which he was influenced by Brook is not easy to assess, partly because they were so young when they started working together. 'At that time he had no specific method that he was following in the sense that he has now. So that if one worked with him now for the first time, one would have to find that one was being influenced by Peter as to method, as to the way of working. But his influence in the early days was simply much more through contact with a very acute, perceptive, imaginative approach towards the plays. In a way working with him was quite traumatic. One was suddenly thrown up against a directorial influence which was so demanding of whatever intellectual powers one possessed – which were so undeveloped – that I suddenly found that the business of being an actor was something quite different from what I had perceived, even as a student.

'I think that hitherto I had been fairly preoccupied with training my equipment, as it were, and relying on my imagination and on what I fondly considered was my intuitive sense of observation about people. Peter made me *think*, which is something quite different, and think in relation to the play as a whole, and the part that the character took in the general pattern of what the author was assembling. But this was actually quite a natural piece of education for me because I was very young at the time, and perhaps if it hadn't happened through Peter it would have happened through somebody else. But it literally shocked one out of any sense of complacency one might have had, and when one is very young and learning a profession, one feels most complacent, I think. Not that one knows everything, but that one's confidence has never been assailed. The more one learns about such work as we do in the theatre, the less one can feel sure of oneself.

'And at this point I encountered Peter and he was the kind of person who delivers shocks to the system, not by calculation, but just by confrontation with his intelligence.'

Even then he must have had more sense of the whole than most directors?

'Yes, he did, he did absolutely. He would have a conception of the play at the first reading which to us, at the Birmingham Repertory Theatre, seemed almost impertinent. That anyone so young should presume such grasp. And being a tight-knit group, as every repertory theatre is, we would resent this and we would feel "I don't believe this assumption of grasp". But not for very long. This was the first defensive reaction to the impact of Peter. But it then took perhaps two days for us to realize that his grasp was fully backed up. This was quite a salutary shock to us. I for one was simply aware that I was working with a director who could use what I had to offer but not indulge me at all. I was growing and developing and I suppose I was showing some signs of having resources and reserves, and he probably recognized this, but was very very disciplinarian about it. He didn't ever tell me that I was marvellous. On the contrary, I think he detected a certain laziness in me and tried to correct it.'

So you had a feeling that he was making you use more of yourself?

'Yes, absolutely. Whether he was really interested in doing this or whether this was just the thing that was natural for him in order to get the play that he wanted, whether at that time he was interested in the art of the actor, I don't know. But certainly you could feel him becoming a director of actors rather than simply a director of a play. Actors were perhaps at that time becoming to him very clearly instruments that he could draw from – not manipulate, but use in the best sense.'

The voice Scofield uses in conversation is quite different from any you remember from his performances. 'Well I suppose it bears very little relation really to what I do on the stage. Or it seems to. Probably I've never quite used the voice that I speak with in everyday life. But then who does? One has to expand in order to enlarge one's voice in order to be heard. It's difficult to describe because I have no system. With every play that I do I try to start absolutely from scratch, so that I will begin rehearsal in a very neutral way, vocally. It isn't a hit or miss thing so much, it's a question of the voice growing out of what becomes apparent to me about the kind of man I'm pretending to be. It's possible that I may begin to feel like him in my face or in the way that I sit down, or in the way that I walk, before I come to sounding like him. Or it can be the other way. There may be just one line in the middle of the second act, say, and suddenly it will become clear to me that this is the way for this particular man to say that line and this is the kind of voice that emerges from that understanding. That's the beginning and then everything begins to match up to that tiny piece of insight.

'I think it's nearly always the voice which leads me – and I think a lot of actors – towards other characteristics of the person one pretends to be. And I think the reason it's the voice is that it's the spoken thought which is given to us by the writer. I mean it's his, the spoken thought that he has asked us to pass on to the audience. This is why it's nearly always the most important thing to feel that your voice is responding to what he's written in a way that makes sense. Other things follow, things that you hadn't planned to do at all, simply because they're the sort of things you'd do if you were speaking in that sort of voice.'

Sometimes this leads to a voice which is quite outlandish, as in *Expresso Bongo*. 'I suppose that was an approximation of my reaction towards people I have come across that lived in that kind of agents' world. And by agents I'm not talking of agents that I have worked with professionally, because theatre agents are very different. I'm talking about a kind of agent – the pop singer's agent – that in fact I haven't very much experience of. In fact I've hardly met the people in that world at all. But it doesn't take much to find the parallels in people one does know.

'Though it's a fairly dangerous way of working, because one only has oneself as a source of reference and what one's ears tell one one's own voice is doing, and when one hears one's voice played back on a record, it's a great big surprise. So that it's easy to see why one can be very much disagreed with. What I, for instance feel is the right voice for a particular character, perhaps makes other people think "I don't understand at all. What does he mean by that voice?" Things sound differently to people. Not only does my voice sound different to you from the way it sounds to me, but it would sound different again to someone else.'

This explains something about the way he sinks himself into a character. He does not erase himself, but he is never tempted to use the role as a vehicle for putting his own personality across to the audience. Without being physically protean like Alec Guinness, or a virtuoso with greasepaint and nose-putty like Olivier, he disappears into the role, changing his gestures and gait to fit the character, creating shapes which stay in the mind long afterwards – his narrow, lightweight, mincing Khlestakov in *The Government Inspector*, his broad, bearish Macbeth, his gaunt, gawky, angular Vanya, his square, earthy Lear.

Sometimes the process by which he creates these shapes is touched off by the costume, as happened with Khlestakov. 'The walk and the way I moved was very much dictated by the costume, and I think this is not to be underestimated. One's movement is immensely influenced by a period of costume. But while I was most interested in finding the right voice for that, I never really saw Khlestakov as looking like anything I could put my finger on, or sounding like anything that would make me think "Oh that's what I would like to sound like". I was much more interested in finding in him the means of expressing everything that I knew about pretensions. Because this was a kind of definitive representative of pretension in literature. That character just becomes intoxicated by the success of his pretensions – and also by drink. But this is a lovely, a joyous thing to try and do. Because pretensions are funny, and one observes them so often in a censorious and distasteful way. It's rather nice to be able to put them to good use and be able to make comedy out of them. It wasn't so much a person, because Khlestakov is in a way not really a person. But he represents so much foolishness in us all. That's what I loved.

'I was simply interested in making that kind of behaviour true, whatever kind of person one was being. It probably broadened the character quite a lot. It probably made him pretty unbelievable in a sense. But I do that more and more. I find myself being much more interested in finding in a character something which is common to a lot of people.* I believe that when a writer creates a character of any sort of dimension, he is not specifying how he should look, how he should walk, exactly how he should be, but that he is a kind of person that we can all recognize and find some of ourselves in, see a lot of people that we know – friends – find things you have contact with all the time in life, and make these things clear through the means of the character, not in any sense approximating to human characteristics but by being

*Compare John Wood's remark on p. 59.

absolutely specific. When one thinks for instance of Tolstoy and the kind of characters that he portrayed, he is pretty specific about the way he describes people, but one finds so many people one knows within his characters. But I feel drawn to attempting by means of acting what maybe a painter attempts. I can see in a way that my attitude to acting has changed very much. I become less and less interested in myself in performance and much more interested in what the writer has opened up for me and how I can best illustrate this, almost without feeling that I am present.'

This is not the way most actors function; nor did Scofield start off by functioning like this. He is very clear about the point of arrival at this change of objective. 'The turning point is very precise in my mind: it was when I did a play called *The Power and the Glory* with Peter Brook. It was a whole new experience, because that was a very muddled play – I suppose necessarily so because it was from a very episodic book, and if they had attempted to make a neat play of it much of the wandering feeling would have gone, the kind of nomad quality that the character has, and the kind of contact with all sorts of people. And so this very diffused structure of the play allowed me in a way to wander with it and to find a kind of freedom from not being too bound by precision. Technical precision certainly is a very good thing to learn, but perhaps I found at that point that effective acting was not what I wanted to do. That I didn't want to make effects. But I wanted, as it were, to leave an impression of a particular kind of human being, or create an atmosphere in a scene which an audience would take or leave, to a certain extent, as it wanted to. Not be too definite, not say "This is what this person's like, this is this kind of man, this is what the story means".'

Leaving things open rather than closing them.

'Yes, but it was mostly for me as an experience of liberation in finding myself free, finding that within the security of the character I was playing, I could do anything. It was interesting – it didn't matter what I did. It was like improvising in a sense except that I'm not an actor who could improvise without a script.'

And I wonder whether that's got something to do with a desire for a particular kind of contact with an audience, saying

'Here are the common factors between the character and you'.

'I think so. Because I have a much greater sense of contact with audiences now than I used to have. In fact the contact one has is a very mysterious one. It's absolutely un-analysable, and you can talk about the sense of whether the audience is listening or not, whether they are concentrating or not, whether they're coughing, whether they're laughing, the satisfaction you get from the laughter and the degree of intensity of their concentration and all these things. None of that is very satisfying, but there is one thing that always interests me very much. When actors are in rehearsal, the director takes the place of the audience completely. He becomes the focal receiving point for everything one is doing, every attempt one is making to clarify the play in terms of acting. And then, when the play gets in front of an audience, the feeling is in fact exactly the same as if one were playing to one person. The director has removed himself and because he is not there one is only aware of his influence through what one is doing. But an audience feels like one person, and I have no possible explanation of that except that I think there is something very mysterious that happens to people when they're en masse – a greater or smaller mass – and are concentrating all on the same thing. They have in common what they're watching, but they also contribute to each other in a curious way. And the feeling at the end of the first act, and the feeling at the end of the play from an audience is quite different from when the curtain lifts up. Something unifying happens.'

But he also focuses his awareness on the space. 'I'm always aware of the four corners of the theatre in terms of my own vision. If I'm not, then I think it's fairly clear that they're not going to be aware of what's going on with me. I don't mean I'm thinking about those people, but aware, within my field of vision, of their existence, so that I don't miss anybody, so that there isn't a completely forgotten area that hasn't come within my peripheral vision. In films of course I think unconsciously one is still doing it for an audience. That is, one's still thinking in terms of the consumption of what one's saying and thinking, although they're not there.'

Certain roles, obviously, provide more opportunity than others for the kind of contact with an audience that Scofield now wants. There is a Vanya in every member of the audience, so *Uncle Vanya* provides more opportunity than Osborne's *Hotel in Amsterdam*. 'Yes, very much more because *Hotel in Amsterdam* is essentially a very claustrophobic kind of idea. The whole play is concerned with the obsession of a group of people about one other person at a particular time of crisis, and going round and round this man and this moment of rejection of him. Which is such a very restrictive piece of geography in a sense, one couldn't get away from that central idea at all, so that was really what was important in the play. And it was quite interesting that the character himself was a man who didn't appear. My character was obsessed by him. He in a way was the most interesting character in the play, although he didn't appear. He was a kind of Diaghilev. It might have been the way Nijinsky felt about Diaghilev. He was necessary to the others, but they wanted to feel they could do without him. It's quite a common relationship, I think, not only in the art fraternity but amongst people who employ people. That was interesting about that play. But *Vanya* opens up an enormously wide field of comment about waste and guilt and guilt *about* waste. It says it so beautifully. And it doesn't say anything – that's what's so extraordinary. None of the characters are specifically articulate about the sense of waste they have inside them. Underneath all the commonplaces it's all there. Chekhov was able to choose virtually quite fatuous things for people to say and to indicate beneath them what they are really thinking about.'

Anna Calder-Marshall, who was Sonia in the Royal Court production of *Vanya* described what it was like to find herself playing most of her important scenes with Scofield. 'It takes such a load off acting when the people you're with are just *there*, and they change from night to night and you realize you couldn't do a speech in the same way, because you're getting different things all the time. Some nights I was a bit too soft. It's very difficult at the end because it can be sentimental. One night I was indulgent and I felt I wasn't helping Paul enough. The balance between the two is very delicate.'

Scofield, in turn, praises her capacity for responding freshly

each evening and each moment to the impulses given to her.
'She's an immensely flexible actress in that way and I think
it's because she has got a mind, and she relates and reacts
extraordinarily to the person she's working with. Which
is why she would find what she found, working with me.
I do like to establish a very free kind of open relationship so
that things can be changed on the impulse of the moment.
The tone that comes from somebody else, that you never heard
them do before, can absolutely radically change your feeling
about the next thing that you have to say, and you just allow
it to. She's very open to suggestion in this way. She's really
there. She has the intellect to grasp the moment of a change
like that if something is happening. She can use it and take it
over from there. I found her quite remarkable. She has a very
strong feeling, but she senses when it's exaggerated or false
or unnecessary or redundant. And when an expression of feeling would be one which would do what the audience should
be doing. Sometimes one must hold back feeling, otherwise
the audience is not going to feel it. I think one must hold it
back very very strongly, because what one is trying to
represent as the feelings of a character very easily becomes infused with one's own personal sense of sympathy
with the predicament, and the audience then sympathizes
less.'

*I suppose particularly with somebody like Vanya who is
so sorry for himself.*

'Exactly, and that's all one must show. Not how right he
is to feel sorry for himself. Or what a shame it is. They're
two separate things, the expression of what Vanya feels and
the complete holding back of what *you* feel. You can only
arrive at the expression of what Vanya feels by means of your
own feelings, so that in a way a kind of split has to happen.
Or by means of your own understanding of his feelings, your
own perception. In order to see clearly one has to be able to
feel as well. But then I think one has to make a very very
clear division and not allow one's own feelings to intrude. It's
impossible of course to stop them altogether. But at the same
time one has to make the effort. It's like crying too much and
then audiences don't cry.'

Of course there ought to be nothing unusual about the
flexibility and the sensitivity that Anna Calder-Marshall has

in common with Scofield, or the ability to respond to whatever happens on stage, to create a new set of variations in each performance which slot in with the variations that are occurring in other people's performances. But in fact this kind of spontaneous creativeness is not often found. 'It is very rare. Oddly enough it seems to be a facility that people lose as they get successful. That's a great generalization, because there are some who've got beyond that and through the rocky, shaky time of early success, when either the actor settles for repeating success or is determined to press through to possible non-success, simply in order to grow. And some do do that. But what I think I am trying to say is that usually you find this amongst actors who are beginning – you find this sensitivity to impressions and to influences from the people they're working with, so that there's something reciprocal going on all the time. But when a certain amount of success is achieved, then for safety's sake people are inclined to stand still and try to repeat whatever it was that worked last time. I think this does something which closes the mind to response. Because it's only by being willing to start again every time after whatever it is that you've done, whether it's worked or whether it hasn't worked, whether it's been considered successful or not, it's only by starting absolutely as if that had never happened that one can remain open to influences from other people.'

Scofield tries never to repeat himself and never even to repeat the same method of approach. His intention is to start on each new characterization without preconceptions, to go to the first rehearsal of each production without knowing how he is going to set about working. 'Sometimes things happen very fast and sometimes one has to take one's time. I'm very careful not to let any kind of pattern emerge too soon. I also learn a lot from other people when I'm working with them. If I'm very sure early on of what I want the final result to be, then I can sense that quite soon. Of course it happens more often that one isn't sure. But sometimes it happens I am. I was very sure right from the beginning of *Government Inspector*. I knew what it should be almost from the first reading, and I was right – whether it was good or bad I don't know, but it worked.'

Many actors are already thinking about effects they want

to make in performance before they even go into rehearsal. But just as a director like Brook will devote the early part of a rehearsal period to digging into the material without planning how any discoveries will be used, so will an actor like Scofield. 'I find that energy in rehearsal, the early part of it, has got to be devoted entirely to thinking, and that my equipment – my voice, and what I'm doing, sitting, standing, or whatever – has got to be completely in abeyance, forgotten about, lost. I don't waste any energy on that because I don't yet know what I'm doing with them, so I must leave them to be idle and get on with it up here. It's only gradually and in the last stages of rehearsal that one can use the kind of physical energy that is needed in a performance, because then the whole man, as it were, of the character is functioning along the right lines.'

If actors can be divided according to whether their prevailing interest is in style or in accuracy, Scofield's is unequivocally in accuracy. 'I'm not drawn towards expression of any sort of beauty in the theatre, beauty of line or movement or voice or anything.' In a Shakespearean part he would never give priority to speaking the verse as verse. When he played Macbeth in Peter Hall's production at Stratford-on-Avon in 1967, he started by breaking the verse up into very short phrases with pauses between them that seemed arbitrary and became rather distracting. But by the end of the run at the Aldwych (April 1968) he had settled down into a far steadier reading of the part, breaking the natural rhythms only in the 'Tomorrow and tomorrow and tomorrow' speech, where the staccato he introduced served both to make it seem less of a set piece and to illustrate the disintegration in Macbeth's mind. The broken rhythm in Scofield's speaking reflected the changes that had overtaken Macbeth's capacity to think in a straight line.

'With words like those, that carry so many strong tunes with them, you have to fight to find the freshness of them. And you have to make them *yours* in some way. And I'm prepared for it to sound ugly as long as it has a kind of fresh meaning. Of course I would rather do justice to the poetry than do that, but if I found myself speaking the poetry beautifully, or getting near to doing so, or in any way being preoccupied with speaking the poetry beautifully, and found that it was not really alive, I would rather sacrifice the verse. Because one's going to lack something somewhere. I don't imagine that a performance of mine of Macbeth can have all its aspects filled in. And I would rather miss that kind of perfection, in order to aim for something that was recognizable as the truth about that play, in a fresh way. Not fresh for the sake of being fresh, or fresh for the sake of being original, but just in order to make people hear it as if for the first time.'

Working on *Lear* with Brook, Scofield had found that his performance, like the production as a whole, always seemed to have existed in embryo from the beginning of rehearsals. 'It grew, and there was a lot of very very hard work done on it, but there was nothing that had to be scrapped.'

Whereas in Macbeth you had to recognize false starts and make radical changes in approach during rehearsal work?

'Yes, it was very much more difficult, that. I never had a very clear sense of the wholeness of the play. I grasped the play, in a sense, in my mind, but I never felt the end of it at the beginning of it. I, as it were, stepped from ice floe to ice floe, with a great sense of insecurity and danger, but that was my fault. I never somehow succeeded in making a whole character.'

Scofield does not feel that he fits easily into roles calling for military characteristics. Most actors have difficulty with the warrior aspect of Macbeth: Scofield had difficulties too, but there was no sign of them in the performance. 'Maybe if it worked it was because I paid great attention to it. Because I thought perhaps it wouldn't come too naturally. It was a most fascinating and elusive affair, the character. I don't feel I've done it yet. I want to try and get it. It felt really quite passionate, but I can quite believe it didn't really look it. Perhaps it never really emerged.'

I thought it was more passionate at the end of the run.

'Well I think so, I think it had grown, and I think we had grown through a lot of difficulties. Which is always a rather exciting thing to happen, because if one does find the hiccough at the initial stages of the opening performance, it's very exciting when the actors themselves, through working together, eventually work through to finding a kind of unity. I think it was perhaps unity that it lacked. But how a particular group will react to a particular play can never be predicted, especially one of the huge plays like that.'

In *Hamlet* there is the same problem of bringing the meaning freshly to life theatrically. 'It's hard to keep away the mechanical processes of taught interpretation, however freshly one tries to think about it. Probably the first time I played Hamlet, I had something of this problem, and I didn't really resolve it the second time I played it either. It was maybe fresher the first time. It was the second time that was more difficult and the problems of the play became more painful in a way, more painfully difficult to try to solve. I found myself almost out of sympathy with the character, and I found that the dominant note of revenge, of vendetta as it were, that's in the play, is something which doesn't really communicate to modern audiences. That you seem to be "carrying on" a great deal. In Sicily perhaps it might strike a more immediate response, but one has to work very hard at that to make an audience sympathize with a planned revenge. So that he seems to be very self-absorbed, in fact, and that's not what Shakespeare intended at all. What must have been impressive to the audience when it was first done was the family sense, the sense of family pride and the absolute need to avenge his father, which I think eludes a modern audience.'

Scofield is open-minded about the advantages and disadvantages of working in permanent companies like the RSC and the National. In any case, as he says, there is no long-standing tradition of ensemble theatre in this country. 'I think the Moscow Art Theatre, for instance, work in a very different way from the English. They seem to work together for so long that any sense of staleness in their relationship has been long passed and they seem to have developed a very strong, extra-sensory awareness of each other that binds them all together and makes them able to anticipate each other. I think that companies like that are used by their directors in a most remarkable way. I think that they cast actors not in any kind of conventional way, saying it's the right sort of person with the right sort of voice. Because they know their actors so well they know their sympathies, they know the amount of insight an actor has, whether an actor's understanding of human nature can penetrate that area that Chekhov has written. They seem to explore each other a great deal in that way. I suppose we in our permanent companies have not been together long enough.'

In his first appearance at the National, as Voigt in *The Captain from Köpenick*, Scofield had a great opportunity of finding common factors between the character and the audience. 'He seems to represent almost anyone that's ever suffered from bureaucratic restrictions and the kind of callousness that was so very well represented in Gian Carlo Menotti's *The Consul*—people waiting in offices and people ignoring them. And this terrible wearing down of the morale, especially of people who don't have the money and the influence to go swiftly through the bureaucratic barriers, but who are kept waiting on the outside. I suppose this is something that I feel very much in sympathy with and indeed I can't imagine who doesn't. But it's rather nice to have a specific means of expressing the kind of distaste one feels for that kind of officialdom and the kind of advantage that officialdom takes.

'I suppose it can very easily be explained in terms of people wanting power but I think that's a little bit easy – I think probably fewer people want power than one imagines. But it's a complete insensitivity to other people I think mostly, that makes certain types of officials behave in a very cruel way to supplicants, to petitioners, to people just simply wanting a pass, or a passport, or something signed, or something stamped. They're made to feel very small, and are made to wait.

'Of course he's a very particular case, this character, because he's not just the Patient Citizen. He's in fact somebody who has overstepped the bounds of law and has been in prison. He's an old lag, as it were, but a very minor one, a very petty one, someone who simply forged a postal order when he was very young and who got an enormous and very savage prison sentence for it, and when he came out, found it very difficult to go straight again, and did something else minor and went back in again. You know, it was a rut that was impossible to get out of. So in rather a pallid and negative creature, some kind of violence was growing out of a simple human rejection of this kind of treatment. So there is a specific point in the play which is very sentimental – the death of the girl which seems to be what sparks him off into a kind of violent defiance of the powers that be. And from then on it seems he has no doubt. That something very positive must be done before he dies.

So that the means of getting his passport, which is what has been denied him all these years, becomes also a kind of moment of assertion of his own living – that he will do something to be remembered, to be noticed at least.'

I wonder to what extent this kind of consideration is either a conscious or unconscious influence on your choice of parts.

'I can't say that it's conscious because I can't say that I choose such and such a play because of the relevance of its content. One might say it's unconscious but I do consciously – I won't say choose or pick – feel sufficiently drawn towards it to say this is something I would like to do. A kind of human predicament that I recognize, and maybe that I think "Well, I understand that sufficiently to be able to do it justice". And then it becomes exciting because it is something that you can see a clear line of action through.'

But this could work equally with a figure who represented a viewpoint antipathetic to your own?

'Yes, it could, very very easily. It gives one a kind of inner satisfaction if what the character is about and what the play is about is something about which you also feel quite strongly. But it wouldn't make any difference if it were running counter to that current because it would be equally interesting to find what is sympathetic – not necessarily sympathetic because sympathy doesn't matter, but to find an understanding of a viewpoint that one doesn't share.'

The vocal range and flexibility Scofield has developed are enormous. Voigt, Lear, Thomas More in *A Man for All Seasons*, Vanya, Johnny in *Expresso Bongo*, Khlestakov, and Charles Dyer in *Staircase* all spoke in remarkably different voices. 'I had a certain vocal range at the beginning, although I didn't know how to use it, and consequently I was inclined to stick to one area vocally. But I think it was in the first place a conscious effort when I was learning to be an actor, the actually conscious effort of making myself go as far as I could in every possible direction, and being in a way rather fool-hardy and believing that there wasn't any area that I couldn't go to, although that sounds very immodest. I don't mean that I necessarily thought I could do anything. But I thought that I could try. And particularly perhaps in rep. and at Stratford-on-Avon where one was given a wide variety of parts in a short period of time, so that simply to exercise myself I suppose I must have consciously tried to extend my range. But, even then, for a long time, I didn't succeed. I mean there's always an area of range that one just doesn't have anyway. But I went to the first rehearsal of *Venice Preserv'd*, which was directed by Peter Brook, and I did Pierre and at the first reading I saw the possibilities of the character, but something seemed totally missing somewhere in terms of myself doing it. And Peter said to me after that reading "Of course you do know that you're going to have to find a new voice for this". And I went away and thought about it, and I really consciously, almost for the first time in my life, *consciously* decided on a voice, decided on a specific timbre and depth, and during rehearsal set about trying to get it. And I think in the end that I did. I at least know I changed my voice for that part, and felt that it worked, and that was the first time really I ever knew that that was what I'd done. Apart from obvious characterizations, like playing old men, I changed my voice in this instance in order to be able to encompass an area of emotion and a kind of man who was still my own age but different from me. I was quite young at the time and it was a very vigorous character of my age, but my voice wouldn't do. It wasn't right. So I had to find another. And this taught me it was possible. But I haven't since then consciously done this. I haven't since then made this my aim – to change my voice – it's only been necessary for me in order to express what I feel is in a character.'

But I suppose once consciously having done it, unconsciously you go further than you otherwise would.

'Yes, exactly. One is aware of the kind of limit one can try, and so one tries even further than that.'

Macbeth is not his only performance to have grown very substantially during the run. His empirical method of working, his flexibility and his honesty make this kind of growth not at all uncommon. Even his Sir Thomas More in Robert Bolt's *A Man for All Seasons* – one of his most famous performances – had by no means fully matured when the curtain went up on the first night. 'Of the things that I've done, this was perhaps the least well represented at the opening. We hadn't found a way of doing the play, and I know I was very muted. I think that I was kind of hovering in the wings as it were, wondering how to play it. The tentativeness was simply because I couldn't see where I must commit myself.

'The voice on that was indeed a great problem to me, because the strength of conviction involved in that character was such that there was one point at rehearsal when I was sounding like Tamburlaine the Great or something. Because by putting that amount of strength, literally, vocally, one became kind of a booming, bellowing hot-gospeller, just simply trying to put the full force into the man's convictions. This was clearly quite wrong, and what was missing was the total discipline and restraint of the man, and it was possibly at that point that we opened. And then there was much too much discipline and restraint, though in the end I found a balance.

'And I suppose I attempted to interpret the kind of legal way of thinking of the man in terms of a sort of dryness. This may have in its initial stages been a little too dry. I think that possibly the only way to arrive at the right kind of voice for Thomas More was through the way he thought, which was as a man of law. And a man of law doesn't necessarily speak in a dry and restrained way, but that's a way to find it. And then the humanity of More will be added to it and the appetite for life which he had will be added to that and finally one arrives at all the colours being there in the voice.'

What was it like transferring that to the screen?

'It was very exciting, because I think for the first time I felt that I knew what I was doing in a film. And this was only because I had a large knowledge of the play and the character, and was not starting from scratch and was able to meet the technical demands of film-making, which I was comparatively new to, with a predigested knowledge from beginning to end, a sense of the development of the man, of the story, of the whole thing. So that wherever I was shunted to in the picture – I mean one day one might be doing a scene towards the end of the film before one had been through the development which led to the man's being in that particular state – for the first time this was not a worry to me, because I had it all inside me. I could switch from place to place, although in fact Fred Zinnemann who directed it didn't do that very much. He shot it to a remarkable extent in continuity.'

Without being in any doubt that he has learnt a certain amount from films and television that has been useful on the stage, he is sure that he has gained more from his work on the radio. 'It's not just the question of vocal effect, it's a question of absolutely truthful thought, which if it's not there on the radio is very apparent. And I suppose in the same way, working in front of a camera does make you simply think in a totally concentrated way. But I think one has to think in a totally concentrated way in the theatre. I suppose it's possible not to, without it showing too much. But if you *do* use that kind of concentration in the theatre, that shows.'

But of course concentration is only one of the elements necessary to an effective performance. Ever since he played Henry V at Stratford-on-Avon in his first season there, he has been 'terribly aware of the kind of energy that was needed in a large theatre like that. The theatre in those days seemed larger than it is now, because the stage was further back because of the orchestra pit and one seemed very isolated from the audience. It seemed like an immense effort to communicate at all. It's a much better theatre now. And this of course is a lesson that all actors have to learn at some time. It is extraordinary how, when energy is not being consciously expended, a performance dies. And I think that you have to come to learn this, and I think it's quite hard to learn – that you can't just sit back and think and be true. One has to generate and push through one a constant current of energy, through what you're saying and doing. Even on the evenings one is tired, one must. In fact what I think an actor very often finds is that this current of energy comes through more strongly when he is tired, because it's not springing from any natural vitalities, it's having to be forced through tiredness.'

However much a performance varies in other ways, the supply of energy must remain the same. 'When a performance changes by emphases and shifts, by means of spontaneous thinking – because one is thinking freshly and differently, one hopes, all the time – emphases do change, and I think this can only be sustained if the energy is constant. It varies during the course of the play in that some moments of a play are more relaxed than others, but relaxation doesn't mean a cessation of energy.'

One of the qualities that distinguishes the really creative actor from actors who are merely competent and effective is his ability to keep himself and his performance in a state where

freshness, spontaneity and invention are always possible. This
is easier, naturally, when he is working in a repertoire. 'With
one play on Tuesday and Wednesday and another on Thurs-
day and Friday the two plays mainly benefit from this because
one comes very very freshly from one play to another. In a
long run in the commercial theatre, it's possible to keep spontaneity, but it's very hard work because I think the human
mind does reject repetition, and there comes a point when
it can just say no and refuses to remember. And you don't
remember, and that's very frightening. That's the extreme
result, but in between spontaneity and that refusal of memory,
is a whole area of a fight against being mechanical in any way
– being mechanical because you cannot bring your mind
freshly to exactly the same thing every night, night after night,
for twelve months.'

But an actor can also make too many sacrifices for the sake
of working in repertoire and become stale by staying too long
in a company like the National or the RSC. Scofield has done
stints with both. 'But I don't like to feel that the theatre is
divided into very sharply segregated fields in which you can
only work in that bit. After all, the English theatre itself has
its boundaries. It's not a vast and limitless field and I think it
should be explored by an actor in every area.'

For an actor like Scofield, as for any real artist, the right
to explore freely is indispensable. He is essentially an actor –
one with no driving urge to direct and none at all to have a
company of his own. Indubitably he is making more of a contribution to the English theatre by keeping himself free than
he would by tying himself down to any institution.

JOHN GIELGUD

~━◦━~

'John Gielgud's strongest impulse,' Paul Scofield has said, 'both
conscious and instinctive, seems to me to be directed towards
form and symmetry, an affirmation of the beauty of language
and the perfection of visual line. An impulse which has been
responsible for more moments of awareness of beauty than I
have found from anyone else in the theatre. His chief weapon
is for speaking, which seems in the same instant to search for
form and to rest in a civilized certainty. This is his area of
total authority, and the tangles of relationship, the psychological inquiry, and the small change of human behaviour have
not I think provided material for him as an actor. He will
smooth the odd ugly angle into something symmetrical.'

One of the most extraordinary things about Gielgud's
career is the variety of the parts he has played in his fifty
years on stage, while doing so little to change either his
physical appearance or the sound of his voice. Within the limitations of his range he has great suppleness, but his acting
does not depend at all on impersonation. Talking in his
characteristically self-disparaging way, he says 'I think that
really I'm apt to be Richard II or Hamlet or whatever I do,
and if you've seen me in those parts and think I've really succeeded in those parts, those parts have seemed to permeate
my personality. But you cannot avoid your own particular
mannerisms recurring to some extent over the years, though
Coquelin is supposed to have altered himself completely in
every part he played.'

One characterization in which Gielgud did substantially
transform himself, both physically and vocally, was the Shylock in his own 1938 production of *The Merchant of Venice*.
Laurence Olivier considers this to be one of the best performances Gielgud has ever given, but the critics were hostile
and he became unhappy about it. 'I got very bad notices as

Shylock. I was terribly put down by it, because I thought I'd done it well. There were some beautiful performances and I thought it was a good production, but somehow or other I couldn't find Shylock at all. I thought I had a good make-up. Whether people didn't want to see me in that part, or whether it was because of the Nazis or because I didn't think about it enough I don't know. I do remember that it seemed a very fragmentary part in which you couldn't get very much from the other people. Bassanio and Antonio seemed such stooges in the first scene, and then you have the scene with Tubal, another stooge, the scene with Launcelot and Jessica, and they're stooges, and finally the trial scene, in which I did think I made a great mistake in the staging. Funnily enough I tried to get in that scene rather the same thing that presumably Jonathan Miller achieved in his 1970 production at the National Theatre – making it rather drab and matter of fact. And I had a rather simple set too – white pillars and brown curtains, and Antonio in a funny little dock, and no sort of splendour. And I remember thinking afterwards "Oh what a mad mistake I made". Because I had seen Ellen Terry do it on tour – just the trial scene – with a kind of imitation of the old Lyceum production, with a lot of colour and splendour. And I suddenly thought "I'm sure that Shakespeare must have meant this scene to be very spectacular and splendid." Because it's such high melodrama that if you try and reduce it to hum-drum terms, it doesn't seem to work. It's like destroying the scale of Dickens. It's a very highly coloured scene. In fact I think the whole play is. The old production of Irving probably had a kind of grand old-fashioned ceremony that was very suitable to the play.

'Of course I'm very old-fashioned. I shall never forget seeing Ellen Terry come on in that red dress, on the pier at Brighton, entering with wonderful flowing strides, with a book under her arm. It impressed me tremendously, whether because she was a great actress, or old and famous, and besides that she was actually my great aunt. I believed it all of course, but then I was only twelve. I can't imagine what the scenery was like really. But there was a sort of grandeur about it all. You know if you go to Venice and you've seen the Doge's Palace, you can't really have a little committee room on the stage. Shakespeare must have imagined it even more splendidly than we did, and we all know what the court of Elizabeth was like – gallants sweeping about and all those grand clothes – I don't think you can belittle all that in the theatre. I think you are throwing away such an enormous card in your pack if you do. Not real gondolas or any of that realistic nonsense, but that's where Craig was so marvellous in his drawings for *Venice Preserv'd* and the designs for *Henry V* – there was always a marvellous proportion and space – very simplified, to draw attention to the figures or to the heights or to the contrast of the heights and the figures – not a lot of niggly detail. Also he has big curtains and high doorways that you can come through easily. One only has to look at Venice or even at Hampton Court. You either came in through a tiny door because you were coming out of prison, or you came through great double doors that were flung open, and you walked in as if you were seven foot high. And these mystiques are things that the theatre has cherished and lived on for four or five or six hundred years, and it seems to me rather mad to throw them out. Because there is a way – if you have the right eye and the right designer – to use the essentials of them today without being either cliché or commonplace.'

The unfavourable reaction to his Shylock may have helped to steer Gielgud towards 'straight' rather than 'character' acting in his subsequent career. Reactions to some of previous characterizations that had depended on disguise (like Noah in Michel St Denis's production of Andre Obey's play) had indicated that his public preferred to see him on stage looking like himself.

And in the whole of your career since, you've never disguised yourself in the same way as you did as Noah and Shylock?

'No, I suppose I haven't. Well, in the last few years it's been very unfashionable. We did argue about whether I should wear a moustache or not wear a moustache as Harry in David Storey's *Home* because I didn't wear any make-up or any disguise of any kind. So that it's curiously happened that ever since Enid Bagnold's play *The Last Joke* I haven't had to alter myself in any way really. And I think that has helped one to be more true to oneself. Anyway, I've never thought impersonation to be one of my talents. I think it went well with Noah because that was a tour de force: people were impressed that I could do it at all. When I did half try it in *The Maitlands*, the audience wouldn't take it at all, and I wasn't any good either. I altered myself a bit in *The Cherry Orchard*. With Wolsey after the first night of *Henry VIII*, Michael Benthall said "Oh you made a terrible mistake not to be fat," and at first I had hardly any make-up on, and that wasn't any good. When I put more on and padded my body, I think I was rather more effective. I tried not to play for sympathy, to make him more gross and a little more common. But perhaps you can play Wolsey and get away with it as a sort of High Churchman, except that the public knows more about those parts now than they did in the Irving days. Maybe they did know he was a butcher's son, but they hadn't read all those biographies and details, which the ordinary public now knows about, so I think they would be less likely nowadays to accept an aristocratic Wolsey, which certainly isn't really right. I think Laughton should have played Wolsey rather than Henry VIII. He would have been wonderful.'

There is a point of view from which all acting is just an elaborate game, an adult prolongation of the childish pleasures of dressing up in fine clothes and pretending to be someone else. Occasionally actors halt in their tracks to ask themselves what they have been doing with their lives and whether it has all been worthwhile. But these moments are rare, and most of the time most actors would say, as Gielgud says, 'I can't imagine how one could live otherwise.'

He is interested in the extent to which success depends on ability to concentrate. 'All arts and crafts, like sports, demand enormous concentration, and I've never had good concentration at all, but I do naturally try to concentrate on the one thing I am really interested in. But I've always been very sluggish about training myself to be concentrated. I imagine if you're a clever businessman or golf-player or boxer or cricketer or a dancer, you devote half your life to sheer physical slogging and discipline and training to achieve concentration. We don't have enough of this in the theatre. The ordinary person who isn't an actor learns to concentrate mainly through application. Even a man who sits at a desk or works in a bank. But even when I was in dramatic school I used to slink out of all the things I didn't like, just as I slunk out of playing games or swimming at school, and I concentrated on getting out of these irksome things in order to do other things I wanted to do more. In the same way I avoided trying to learn fencing or voice production, elocution – all those things I shirked, because I thought "I can do them my own way and get away with it." It's quite easy (if you're fairly sly) to keep working hard, but only at the things you do most easily, which of course isn't really the way to become good, unfortunately.'

He was lucky, of course, with what he had inherited – a Terry voice from his mother's side of the family, and from his father, an innate musicality, including a gift for playing the piano by ear. 'I never had any trouble with breathing, and when people began to tell me I spoke affectedly, I worked hard to simplify my diction, and to appreciate the phrasing and the actual shape of sentences and words. I never had any difficulty with that, but perhaps that's from a musical sense, which I always had very strongly. It wasn't ever a trouble to me but a pleasure and, when a thing is pleasure as well as part of your work, of course you persevere.

'They used to hold my diaphragm and make me do breathing exercises and I always thought "Oh, nonsense." I showed off dreadfully in my speaking of verse. In fact that was the great fault of my acting for a number of years, that I was very vain about the fact that my diction and my voice were praised and admired. But then on the other hand I've been told I was inaudible in nearly every part I've played in my life. And I tell people that and they say "Oh, you are affected, you with the great silver voice that's heard in the remotest corners of the earth." And I say "Well if I'm not extremely careful I drop my voice at the end of sentences like everybody else does." You've got to be quite cunning to throw your voice in the theatre so that every word is heard, and I worried for many years about my self-consciousness and affected way of walking and standing on the stage.

'I've never played a low-life part – which perhaps is rather lucky – because I don't think I could ever succeed with accents or dialects. I haven't a natural gift for mimicry or accents. I've never even played a Frenchman. I did play with an accent in something. But I sort of invented it. It wasn't a real accent.

Something I did on the wireless, I think. Or maybe it was in *The Last Joke*. I had a sort of accent in Shylock which I invented for myself. I have never studied accents, and I have no languages, which is rather a pity because I'm sure I could have learnt if I'd been forced to. My eldest brother spoke perfect French. But I have a good accent and I think I could have spoken French much better than most English people do. Like Churchill, most Englishmen think it's rather effective to speak French with a terrible British accent.'

Another gift he always had was a great visual flair. As a schoolboy he did a good deal of sketching, and at one time the theatrical career he planned for himself was as a designer. As a director he has been able to work very closely with his scenic and costume designers. But as an actor he has had little help from scenery. 'When I was young I always thought the scenery would be so helpful. One of the last times I saw Craig I said in a rather jocose way "Oh I was so disappointed because I always thought it would be so inspiring to play in front of wonderful scenery. But of course when one is on the stage oneself, one never sees the scenery as it is always behind one!" And he said blandly "Oh my dear boy why don't you have mirrors put at the back of the theatre? They would reflect the scenery, and that would inspire you." And I remember that actually happening in Toronto when I was playing Hamlet and there were mirrors all the way round the back of the stalls, and I had to have them all covered up, because I saw five reflections of myself during the soliloquies, and I couldn't concentrate at all.

'But if you are a director as well as an actor you do see the scenery, and the whole picture much more often than ordinary actors do. Even though one is in front of it when one is acting, one can still visualize the grouping one has arranged. As a rule I find that most actors don't rush in front the moment they aren't in a scene and see what the director is doing. But I always do, because I am very aware of grouping and the pattern of the play from the front. And this way I feel I know better how to fit my own performance in when I join the other actors.'

Another inherited gift was the ability to shed tears at will. Weeping comes so easily to him that often he has to restrain it. 'In Gordon Daviot's *Richard of Bordeaux*, in the last scene of self-sacrifice, the less I gave way to tears myself, the more moved the audience was. Ellen Terry is said to have been able to play the fool for the other actors' benefit even while she was openly weeping her way through a pathetic scene. My mother was, like all her family, extremely emotional as an audience or when reading aloud, though – as I am, too – surprisingly stoical in life during an emergency or emotional crisis. In Shakespeare especially, as was the case with Ellen Terry, I've always had difficulty in restraining easy tears, both in the voice and the eyes, but the deliberate use of this ability, properly controlled – after a certain amount of over-indulgence at rehearsals, and sometimes in performance too – has been of great value to me in parts like Hamlet, Leontes and Richard II, in the scene with the priest in Graham Greene's *The Potting Shed*, in *Home* and once or twice even in comedy parts like the Headmaster in Alan Bennett's *40 Years On*, when a sudden moment of real feeling was required. But audiences are inclined to be over-impressed with actors who really weep; when I once said to Edith Evans "I've learnt exactly the word to start weeping on and the word to stop weeping on," she said "Ah, you're learning to be a good actor". She never milks a scene herself, but in *The Chalk Garden* and in *The Late Christopher Bean*,* she opens the shutters and shows you her heart – then closes them again quickly before she can over-indulge the emotions either of herself or the audience.

'Edith Evans has influenced me a lot. The audience may influence her timing but she resists any temptation to woo them. She moves very little. Even as Millamant she managed to give the impression of a fascinating coquette without much gesture or movement, so that her few moments of action were the more significant.'

Like her, Gielgud has given many of his best performances in classical comedy – Shakespeare, Congreve, Sheridan and Wilde. Here the technical knowledge that he has acquired as a director has been inseparable from his achievements as an actor. One of his greatest comedy successes was as Joseph Surface in Tyrone Guthrie's 1937 production of *The School for Scandal*, though this got off to a very bad start on the first night. 'I remember that I sort of pawed the ground and

*An adaptation by Emlyn Williams of René Fauchois's *Prenez garde à la peinture*.

went on, and then a terrible thing happened. I dried up on my very first line, and had to take it from the prompter. I was terribly nervous and my mind was a complete blank. It's the only time it's happened to me in the theatre, so I was in a frenzy. I had a beautiful costume, I looked very good and I think the few things Guthrie had said to me were rather helpful, and I made the hypocritical Joseph agreeable and rather attractive. The production was quite a success, although I thought a lot of it was very misguided. *The Times* rightly said that the curtain call looked as if we had all gone to the Russian Ballet, and actually it was more carefully rehearsed than anything else in the play. There was an enormous sofa Guthrie had got from some great house and we all bounced up and down on it. This got a lot of laughs, but killed the dialogue. I had a very strong sense then in that play, and later in *The Importance of Being Earnest*, and in *Much Ado* and in *Love for Love*, that in comedy the distance of people on the stage from one another is one of the vital things. And it's something that must have changed very much, because in the days of candle lighting, everybody had to play very much dead front. It does depend enormously on how the furniture is placed, how wide the stage is, and how much ground you have to cover when you move and when you keep still. All this affects the way that comedy is flung from one character to the other and the way one player feeds and the other takes.

'When I was brought in to direct *The Heiress*** at the last minute – which was a great moment for me, to gain the confidence of a very depressed company of actors very late in rehearsals – I realized at once that the man who had preceded me as director had completely missed the point about those rather sententious Henry James scenes, in which it was essential that people sat on the stage and talked at a certain distance from one another, either close or far. But if they were standing throughout a scene of talk, you felt they were in a sort of waiting-room, that at any moment they'd rush off stage to catch a train, and the audience simply couldn't listen.

'In *The School for Scandal*, it's obvious that the scandal scenes are meant to be played on small chairs and sofas from which people simply throw the ball from one to another across the stage. But if everyone is crowded together, as we were in

*An adaptation by Ruth and Augustus Goetz of Henry James's *Washington Square*.

Guthrie's production, on a big settee, cheek by jowl, you can't convey a real effect of witty conversation or give the audience breathing space to be amused by it. In a real party it's very important how you sit with people. If you're talking intimately, or if you're talking to amuse a crowd, if you're being witty, in a circle or at a dinner table, then the *placement* is very important. I always remember Lady Cunard. When I dined with her at the end of the war at the Dorchester she used to have a big round table and put eight or ten people round it, but I noticed the tremendous care she took in placing the guests. A clever hostess knows where the wittiest person should sit and where he's going to dominate best. And which man and which woman on the right of him are going to be the best balance for one another to get the conversation going.'

Gielgud's habit of wandering out into the auditorium during the rehearsal of other actors' scenes stood him in good stead during the nerve-wracked rehearsals of David Storey's *Home* in 1970. 'We felt so exposed sitting at the front of the stage at that table all through that long opening scene. And then I saw the scene in the second act between Ralph and Dandy Nichols from the front, and realised at once, sitting in the auditorium, that there was a kind of third dimension the moment I was away from it, of which playing on the stage I was completely unaware.

'This discovery immediately gave one more confidence. I didn't feel so bare and desperate, or that the scenes wouldn't hold. Lindsay Anderson had done wonders with the few moments of movement in the play. In the last scene, after I had sat between the two women and the table had been taken away, I came down a few steps to the front and Ralph went up to the back, the effect was very striking, though it was impossible for the actors to judge that for themselves. We just had to move as the director told us. I've had battles sometimes with actors and actresses when I've been directing them, because they didn't want to move on a certain line, or they wanted to sit down on a certain line, and in a conventional play the actor has a very strong instinct about that. But in a new kind of play like *Home,* although we continually did say "Can I stay still so long? Can I get up?" the director invented all of the moves, of which there were very few, and he once said towards the middle of rehearsals "Don't ever move on your instincts. When you feel you want to move on a certain line, always delay it. Either do it a little before or a little after, because it gives this kind of oblique suggestion of not being quite right in the head. Don't move on a line as you would in a conventionally constructed play in which you're going to make a point."

'I was very worried when he said "Now don't listen to the others, turn your back and look at the sky". I said "Won't it kill the points that they're making in the front of the stage?" Because one's whole training as an actor is never to move when somebody else has got a good line. And no one else must move when you have a good line. In Storey's play we could break all the old rules, and it was terribly interesting, but you had to trust the director that it would be all right, not disturbing. There was so little movement that any move was noticeable and important. I had to cross the stage several times right in front of the characters who were speaking, which I would never have presumed to do in another kind of play. In a formal play or in Shakespeare it's absolutely essential that you don't draw attention to yourself at the wrong moment. In *Home* everything was so compact and there were so few of us that it was essential to keep the shape and balance and tone exactly.

'What I liked so much about Jocelyn Herbert's set for *Home* was that it had the beauty of a Craig without his tendency to dwarf the actors. It was wonderfully simple and that white light was splendid too. In Peter Shaffer's *The Battle of Shrivings* and in *Home* we played under strong white lights – pretty trying when we had to look into them all the time. But the actors were lit superbly. Until ten years ago all actors demanded footlights. Alfred Lunt and Lynne Fontanne wouldn't appear without them. On tour they even took a set of footlights along with them in case they weren't otherwise available. Women always wanted Surprise Pink in the lights because they believed it made them look younger. Now we wear no make-up, there are no footlights and we have blinding white light which throws no shadows. Hours I used to spend in theatres when I was directing, trying to get shadows away from the backcloth. I've sat twelve hours in a theatre trying to light a play, because I don't really know anything about it technically and I had to do it by trial and error. But in *Shrivings* and *Home*, which were marvellously set and lit, there was hardly any change of lighting during the performance. What an enormous revolution in every department has come about in the last ten years!'

'*Well this is Brecht's influence. He used open white light.*'

'Yes, I remember it very well when I saw *Trumpets and Drums* in Berlin in 1955. Of course in the old days you always lit your play yourself if you were the director. Komisarjevsky was a great master of lighting – I learned much from him. Now a lighting expert is nearly always specially engaged and even at the Court there is a lighting box at the back of the auditorium. All the modern theatres, schools, as well as the Vic and Stratford, have now got lights not only on the stage and at the front of the house, but also a lighting box in which the operator sits, in touch with the prompt corner. So between the two you can pretty well ensure that no serious mistake is made. So that the technicians can see and correct at once any mistakes that are made. In the old days, on tour, you would have to relight your production every time the play moved to another provincial city. You would go on to a big scene in a Shakespeare play, and the important light wasn't on, and you were playing in pitch darkness, and nobody on the lighting board could see what was missing. There's a famous story of Alec Guinness in his *Hamlet* at the New. They had put in a new Pre-set board the day before, which went wrong on the first night, and every cue worked one cue late. So that in the first scene, it was bright daylight for the night scene and then for Claudius's court it was pitch dark. No ordinary lay person realizes what disastrous effect it has if the stage management and lighting should fail.'

Gielgud was full of admiration for Lindsay Anderson's work on *Home*, particularly over the cutting. 'I wouldn't have had the faintest idea what to cut, and he finally cut, I think, nearly ten minutes. Storey was very very quiet, and Lindsay would say "I think these three lines should come out." They're such little lines, and they're all so tenuous, and one would think it wouldn't much matter if this line came out or that line, or you didn't say "Oh yes" for the tenth time. But Lindsay seemed to know exactly how long each passage would sustain without becoming boring. Quite a lot of very good jokes were lost but I think the cuts were exactly right. The play is beautifully short. Of course silly people said to me "It's lovely, but why can't you have a part that gives you more opportunity to speak?"

'You can never please audiences completely. They prefer you to be the way they liked you before. I've come to the conclusion that there is a great nostalgia in audiences – especially with middle-aged people. As they themselves get older, they don't want us to get older on the stage because we reflect for them their own youth and enthusiasm. And when we come on looking as old as they are, without make-up, without disguise, without any panache, and in a "failure" part like the men in *Home*, or like Chekhov's Ivanov, they're apt to be disappointed. They go to the theatre to see us restore their taste for romance and sympathy and poetic abandon and emotion. And if one no longer plays that kind of part, however good they may think you, they're slightly disappointed. On the other hand you may be making a new public of younger people, who perhaps would never have liked you in your old romantic roles.

'*The Ages of Man** got rid of much of my romantic past. And *Home* was a marvellous chance. I can't imagine any of the actors of Ralph's and my standing being offered a play like this (or accepting it) even twenty years ago. Olivier did a great service to the Establishment actor by going to the Royal Court in John Osborne's *The Entertainer* and Scofield afterwards in *Vanya*. I don't suppose the Court would have offered *Home* to Ralph and me unless they'd had those actors to play there, because they would think we wouldn't be interested enough to take less money and appear in this kind of play. Of course we were both afraid of making a mess of it and spoiling our reputations. Neither of us were sure which of the two men's parts we should agree to take. Tony Richardson, who'd read it very quickly and was wild about it, said to me "I think you ought to read both parts and see which one comes out the best for you". But I hardly liked to suggest this. So I said to Ralph "Well which part?" He said "Well I want to do the one with the conjuring tricks". And I said "All right, fine. Then I'll play the other one". And although I'd read the play a couple of times I didn't yet realize how frightfully terse my

*A one-man show based on George Rylands's Shakespeare anthology.

part was. And when we had the first reading, and he had a good many fairly long speeches and I had nothing but monosyllables to answer, I thought "I must be mad, I'm going to be the poor old stooge. There's no part at all, perhaps I ought to give it up". And then Ralph got frightfully depressed too and said "I think *I* ought to give it up, I don't think this play is strong enough". We had fearful doubts, and Lindsay Anderson kept very quiet and so did Storey, though they must have seen us going through all these alarming doubts. We both felt that after a week we could still retire gracefully without causing too much havoc, and they could get somebody else. Of course, until we knew it, we couldn't act it. We stumbled along, saying our strange lines over and over again. I think it was very trusting of us, because you see we were all old stagers – the two actresses felt the same. And it was very clever of the director to produce enough confidence in us to get over that first bridge of acute suspicion which we all had with such an unusual text.

'It's a marvellous invention when at the opening of the second act the boy comes on and wrestles with the table. So strikingly physical after the stillness and quietness of the whole of the first act. And the way the furniture is gradually moved away to make the feeling of everything being taken away from the characters towards the end.'

There was a great deal about the play that the actors could not understand. 'We kept on asking Storey about the background. "What does this refer to?" And we kept on inventing our own reasons for things we mentioned that seemed to have no specific bearing on the play. For instance I say, looking off-stage, "Eyes in the back of your head. Won't do that again in a hurry, will he?" And Ralph answers "I had an uncle once who bred horses." Ralph had the idea that there was really a horse that kicked someone, off-stage. Well, you can't be sure of conveying that to the audience, but it was fun to think of it. Because it gave us a reason for saying it. But Storey wouldn't explain. He said "Well perhaps that's it". He wouldn't commit himself. And the difficulty was that everything we had to say could be either fact or fantasy, and neither we nor the audience, nor the characters themselves really knew for certain. So we had to invent a secret life for ourselves and it was no good discussing it, because it was private to each character. Some of the jokes in the play are splendid. They're tender, not witty but just charming, like *Alice in Wonderland* jokes.'

Do you find yourself varying much in performance?

'I'm determined not to vary. I don't think I do any more, I'm proud of myself, because ever since *Measure for Measure* at Stratford in 1950, I started to discipline myself and not experiment as I always used to do. And ever since then I've really prided myself that I don't add very much or put in very much or take out very much. I simplify as much as possible. Of course you do play better when the audience is with you. You like them to laugh. Not too much. You need the laughter as a softening, a mellowing. But I never cared in *Home* or in Chekhov plays whether they laughed or applauded or cried. I played much more with the fourth wall down in those plays. And for once, although I dreaded it so in Seneca's *Oedipus* and in *40 Years On*, I found looking out at the house very easy in *Home*. Lindsay said at the beginning "Don't turn your back, don't use the ensemble actor's technique of playing together. Play out. Live your life alone through the play." I found that was not so difficult as I'd feared. And sitting in a relaxed way. I've always *sat* on a stage with a tremendously straight back and my legs stretched out, and used a sort of athletic attack that's always been very tiring. But in the Storey play in a small theatre I learned to relax my body, and concentrate with my mind. It was very much less physically exhausting, and that alone, as one gets older, is rather a relief – not to have to put on make-up, not to have to change your clothes, not to have to play violent scenes in which you're breathless and sweating and exhausted at the end. And to know that by being very quiet you're still holding an audience. And using one's voice realistically but not theatrically. I said "How am I going to say 'Well I . . . Well I . . .' fifty times? If I'm to begin planning set tones and inflections for every repetition, then in a few days it's going to become a terrible sort of gramophone record". Lindsay said "Don't decide how you're going to do it. It'll come out right. Do it like Chopin. It's very flexible". And once I had managed to learn the cues correctly I found I didn't worry. I don't prepare how I'm going to speak. There were a few passages towards the end of the play in which the men had to echo each other. Those

I did grade very carefully, vocally, because I knew they must have a very good crescendo, my voice being higher than Ralph's. Such things we planned very accurately, but for the general trend of the give and take, I just emptied my mind and tried to live my character, and Richardson did the same. We never seemed to fail to contrast each other properly.

'We all tried not to imagine all the time we were mad or to think of eccentric things to do. I did put in a slightly off-beat walk, crossing the paving stones rather oddly. This I was terrified by over-elaborating. But as I've spent all my life trying to stride gracefully across the stage, I thought "If I do this slightly hesitating thing with my feet it should give a valuable effect of slight uncertainty". So I invented my walk fairly late on in rehearsals. And in that tiny theatre you could do so little, that everything made its mark.

What about Oedipus? *Did that vary much?*

'Yes I think it did – the whole production as well as individual performances, even though we had ten weeks rehearsal. It was a very unpredictable and variable emotional experience – just as *Noah* was so many years ago. Almost impossible to play either well, except for one or two rare performances. Some nights they used to say I was very good. All the preparatory work had been agony, and misery, and I really resented it in some sort of way, except that I love Peter Brook, and I always have a feeling that anything you do which you resent in the way of preparation – like learning how to use a billiard cue, or learning languages, or doing exercises – the very fact that you hate doing it must mean that it's rather good discipline and may possibly lead to something good. Like going into training or going on a diet or not smoking or drinking. One's often had one's own way too much and to be forced to make an effort is valuable. I think all the physical work improved my balance and control. There again we never quite knew what Peter was driving at . . . He never showed us models of the set or decided till the last moment what costumes we were to wear. And it wasn't until the whole thing was together and we had the set, the lights and the chorus deployed round the front of the circles. We did weeks of very fascinating exercises, in which I showed up pretty badly. And that was good for me too, because the company was a very young one and I made a bit of a fool of myself, which I think increased their respect for me. But also decreased my respect for myself and made me feel that I could afford to make a fool of myself in front of them all without lowering my prestige. One had to risk looking idiotic, which most leading players avoid at all costs. So as not to be found out. Feet of clay and all that. But the work reduced us all to the same level, which was of great value to me, I think, in the end.

'When I went into *40 Years On* soon afterwards, I had to play in a very relaxed and intimate way, aware of the audience nearly all the time. This would once have terrified me, but I found it comparatively easy, to my great surprise, and attributed my relaxation to the strict discipline of the *Oedipus* work with Brook, which had somehow broken down many of my personal mannerisms and self-consciousness.'

The art of acting is the art of making transitions. To speak a single line arrestingly is nothing: any drama student can do it. A good actor is no more interesting in the effects he achieves than in the connections he builds between them. One of the director's main functions in rehearsal is to help him to avoid clichés in bridging from one thought or feeling to the next. And sometimes within an individual speech. With an actor like Gielgud, few directors have the courage or the ability to be really helpful. 'When you get past a certain point in your career, the trouble is that everyone is too respectful to tell you about your faults. That's why I like Peter Brook and Lindsay Anderson so much. They are never rude but they do tell you. When actors get older, they find it hard, of course, to think of new ways of making transitions. You need someone with a very keen eye who can tell you "I don't want any of those old tricks you've used before".'

Another disadvantage of success is the knowledge that one's mannerisms have become popular. So it becomes a temptation to fall back on them rather than think one's way to a new and difficult transition. 'I think your mannerisms are often what audiences like best. They also help to sustain the agony of repetition. Because you can rely on effects which come very naturally to you as signposts in your performance: "I do this bit here. I put on my tears or I put on my heroic voice. And this will help you to carry the next passage through". You take refuge in what you know will appeal and be effective. Every actor must make certain effects. But the danger is of allowing effects to dominate you, to allow them to become more important than your truths. The "effect" of acting, like the "effect" of painting or anything else, must be something you produce on yourself to make the audience convinced. But if it becomes too consciously a trick, it's apt to become a debit rather than an asset.

'Of course you're always on show, but so you are in life as well. When you go to a party, you can't quite be sure when you're being truthful. I fancy that without knowing it I always study my behaviour in private life for the benefit of my work in the theatre. In quarrels and rages, even in great sorrow or delight, I cannot resist watching all the time to see what I'm doing. I see the stage possibilities in every emotion, situation, conversation. But aren't we all manqué actors? A great hostess or a great diplomat or a great speaker in the House of Commons – they're all speaking what they want to speak but at the same time judging their effects. Shaw must have been tremendous like that. In an after-dinner speech one always tries to cover with spontaneous charm what one hasn't really studied to say. And in interviews and radio talks and television talks I think the only thing to trust to is your own sincerity. But how sincere you really are is a terrible uncertainty, above all to yourself. You try to be sincere, but without knowing it, you colour your words according to the people who are interviewing you, according to the audience you think you're speaking to. Because you've had great experience of dominating an audience, with somebody else's words, and now you have to use your own.'

As a director, Gielgud is notorious for wanting to alter everything he established the previous day. As Peggy Ashcroft has complained, 'He's maddening as a director of course, setting things one day in one way and then the next day arriving and saying "Wouldn't it be fun to try it like this?" I never agreed with him. In fact I could never understand why he wanted to go on using me. And it was years before I had the feeling in a part "Here is something firm that I can hold on to". He's an inspirational director. And an inspirational actor, of course.'

Irene Worth defends his directorial habits. 'I think it's poky and old-fashioned to resent the way he changes his mind in rehearsal. It's right to explore all the possibilities there are, and he finds it refreshing to his imagination. He has tremendous stamina and energy, and he actually requires less physical rest than most people do.'

But Edith Evans found it very distressing, when she was asked to alter what she had been developing. 'I get terribly upset when he wants to change things half-way through rehearsals. Because I've given him what came out of my heart. What the Almighty gave me as a way of earning my living. And when something is half-way there, it's like a child. You can't say "It's not a boy now, it's a girl".'

Harry Andrews says 'I only once lost my temper with him and that was when he tried to make a radical change in my characterization at a very late rehearsal. I stamped my foot and shouted at him. "You know you really can't do that to me. You know I'm not an actor who can take such big changes at the last minute". "Oh yes, Harry, I'd quite forgotten. You are rather slow".'

Ralph Richardson claims to have found the right way of coping with the ceaseless flow of new ideas he has always had from Gielgud over the forty years they have so frequently worked together. 'Directors often think they're found a way to manage actors. I think I've found a way to manage a director, and the way I've worked so happily over so many years with Johnny G. is to pin him down. Johnny's rather like a catherine wheel. He springs out with a thousand ideas. Many of them are extremely valuable and I think I'm rather a good editor for them. He'll say "You come through the door and you go straight up to the chair and you sit down". The next day he'll say "I think you should come down the chimney and you should go up to the window and go out of it". I say "Now Johnny, you gave me a marvellous idea yesterday. I'm not going to change that idea until you give me a better one". Out of this catherine wheel I have a little bit of the skill to find and retain the best of the things he gives, and it adds up to something.'

Until 1972, the last play Gielgud had directed in London was Peter Ustinov's *Half Way up the Tree* in 1967, so he was very pleased, while playing in *Home* on Broadway in 1970, to be offered the new Albee play, *All Over*. "I thought it would be fascinating to do it and I had a very interesting time with

the four fine actresses who played the leading parts. The actual
writing of the speeches all through the play is very fine and
I enjoyed phrasing it, and moving it, and I had no movement
at all, except when it was absolutely necessary. Everyone sat
facing the audience on enormous pieces of furniture and just
spoke the play. Albee was very pleased with that. I thought it
worked very well but the house was too big and people
couldn't hear. We had a fortnight of previews, which were
full, and very controversial, just as they were in *Tiny Alice*.
And then no-one came. The cast went on cut salaries after a
week and the play only ran three more weeks.'

Putting himself into the hands of a new director, as he did
with Robin Phillips for *Caesar and Cleopatra* at Chichester,
Gielgud can be pliable and trusting, though he cannot limit
himself to thinking about his own part. His mind flies up to
take a director's, even a historian's view of the play and the
playwright. *Caesar and Cleopatra* interested him particularly
as being the first play to put modern colloquial dialogue into
the mouths of famous historical characters. He sees *Richard
of Bordeaux* and *Vivat! Vivat Regina!* as being 'in direct suc-
cession' to it. 'Shaw was the most marvellous instrumentalist,
vocally. He knew exactly how a speech should be turned. He
was such a good public speaker himself. Where Phillips was
very good with one was that he checked me when I learned
the speeches too glibly and phrased them well musically but
recited them for their own content and not really to inform
the other characters. I found that more difficult to do on an
open stage than it would be on a picture stage. Where one
might be sitting close or just apart from someone on two
chairs or at a table, there we were with this big stage to throw
the lines across and sometimes we even had to speak without
looking at the person we were talking to, coming down to the
front of the stage and looking out over the audience and
speaking as it were over our shoulders, without turning. It
made the intimate scenes very difficult to play, because one
couldn't get too close to anybody. Caesar was anyway a difficult part because it has quite a lot of gags and a strong comedy
twist to it, and yet he must never fail to convince the audience
that he really is a great man.'

Nearly thirty years previously, in 1943, Shaw had written
to Gielgud, trying to woo him away from *Love for Love*

at the Haymarket to star in the film of *Caesar and Cleopatra*.
'You will have to play Caesar some day,' he wrote, 'just as you
have had to play Hamlet and Macbeth. You owe him to your
repertory.' But Gielgud didn't take this very seriously. 'I must
have been awfully stupid. I think I was so contemptuous of the
possibilities of films, and I'd always had a sort of idea that I
didn't find anything in Shaw that appealed to me very much.
And in 1943 I'd have been too young and in 1971 I was too
old.'

Of course the fact of working on an open stage made it impossible to observe Shaw's stage directions. 'Robin got rather
impatient with the endless and rather spectacular stage directions.
He maintained that Shaw's colour sense must have been at fault,
that he must have been colour blind. He was such a brilliant
auditory man but, judging by the things he seemed to admire
in the stage directions, everything ought to be purple and gold
and great shadows, everything rather Royal Academy. Of
course this was the Edwardian theatre taste, and probably he
wrote the stage directions to please Forbes-Robertson.* But I
wonder what Shaw's own pictorial taste was like. I think he
liked the portraits of himself by Topolski and Epstein but I
don't fancy he had much feeling for modern pictures. And of
course in 1898 the whole thing was conceived to be – you
know – Joseph Harker scenery with enormous gods and masses
of extras. We tried to simplify it. Robin had seized very
much on the idea of an old man creating a woman out of a
little girl – which was, I think, very good, as this girl, Anna
Calder-Marshall, is so suited to it, being so small. She really
looks like a little girl, almost completely asexual, which I'm
sure is what Shaw intended, with Ftatateeta as a Nanny. The
attitudes are Edwardian – the images of childhood and the
mastery in Caesar are basically the Edwardian approach of
children to their fathers. Which is exactly what Shaw must
have felt. In a way the play is a first cousin to *Peter Pan*,
which has an Edwardian jokeyness which we find hard to
accept. It's interesting that Shaw, who never had children—
and nor did Barrie either – could understand this child Cleopatra so well, but that he should have thought of it for Mrs
Campbell or Ellen Terry is so peculiar. Because they were
obviously clever grown-up women. But maybe his attitude

*Who played Caesar and co-directed with Shaw.

towards women was very much more the attitude of a teacher and a father figure than a lover, with his vegetarianism and Jaeger underwear. He couldn't ever have been very attractive physically though he was obviously very fascinating. I think at that time the elder generation had a kind of sedate glamour which modern young people don't find attractive about us old people at all.'

LAURENCE OLIVIER

❧

'Mr Olivier was about twenty times as much in love with
Juliet as Mr Gielgud is, but Mr Giegud speaks most of the
poetry far better than Mr Olivier.' This was Herbert Farjeon's
judgment in 1935 when Gielgud directed, first playing Mercutio to Olivier's Romeo and, later exchanging parts with him.
The rivalry between them was to last for twenty-five years
and critics were incessantly comparing them, championing
one against the other as the greater actor. In his first book
He that Plays the King Kenneth Tynan contrasted them in
terms of Burke's *Enquiry into the Nature of Ideas upon the
Sublime and the Beautiful*, equating Gielgud with the Beautiful
and Olivier with the Sublime. He also wrote 'One thinks of
Olivier in terms of other species, of panthers and lions: one
thinks of Gielgud in terms of other arts, of ballet and portrait
painting'. The contrast between them, he said, could be equated
with the contrast Dr Johnson had drawn between Milton's
ability to carve a colossus out of granite and his inability to
carve heads on cherry-stones. 'For the large, shattering effects
of passion, we look to Olivier; for the smaller, more exquisite
effects of temper, to Gielgud.'

But can it be said that either of the two actors had any
influence, positive or negative, on the other? Olivier is three
years younger than Gielgud and had only seen a few of his
Shakespeare performances by the time they first worked together. Olivier, who was then twenty-eight, was not so much
in danger of imitating Gielgud as of recoiling to the opposite
extreme, going with all the more vigour and determinatior
for the physical and earthly qualities. 'I'd found that Johr
had got a preoccupation with the beautiful and the poetic, ir
those days, at the expense of reality. This is certainly, ha:
always been and probably always will be a valid way oi
approaching Shakespeare. But I've always been much mort

fascinated by the idea of convincing people that something was *real*. It took me some years to understand this. You certainly can't arrive at it by discarding the Shakespeare and pretending it's prose. You have to achieve reality *through* the verse and not in spite of it – and not leaning entirely upon it either, I would say. It's just the structure of the building and you've got to live in it. But what comes out could seem and be real along the line of moments of recognition: "I see exactly what he's feeling now". I think you'd probably find that that kind of conviction is obscured by what one might call an ultra-lyrical rendition of verse, in which case it's become nearer song than speech. And I've thought that John was drifting away from the sort of reality I remember feeling that he had when he started playing Shakespeare. He spoke Shakespeare as if it was his natural way of speaking when he was young. When he played Hamlet the second time in 1933, he certainly spoke it like his mother tongue. He meant every word he said. But by the time we did *Romeo and Juliet* he seemed to me to be a little conscious of his gifts, of music and lyricism. I think he was going through a stage of being aware of what was expected of him.'

Of course the contrast between their two approaches can easily be overstressed. 'I don't turn my back on lyricism myself and he can be perfectly real when he wants to be.' But the fact that Gielgud's approach to Shakespearean verse was having such a strong tidal pull not only on the other actors in the *Romeo* company but on the profession as a whole made Olivier strike out in the opposite direction. 'It made me sort of rebellious. It made me think that Shakespeare was now being handled in a certain way and because of the extremely strong influence that any man of John's power and gifts would have, all the company would be going that way, so that when I entered this company, I rather cut across it, thinking in my innocence that they'd say "Ah, this is the real one". But of course it never works like that. I wasn't deliberately trying to scupper the fleet. I was trying to make a success, but I was certainly trying to make it in my own way. I think John, in a way, secretly perhaps, rather leant towards my sort of naturalism. But it didn't alter his own convictions about it at all. In fact I saw him going a little further into the expected field of florid elocutory renditions when he was playing Mercutio after he'd started to rehearse Romeo. By that time he had settled for *almost* singing it – which I didn't like. As soon as I see someone acting in Shakespeare and singing with a tremulo in his voice, I just want to go out, because he's not trying to persuade me that anything real is going on at all. He's just saying "Listen to my beautiful voice" and "Do listen to this glorious cadence I'm about to give you now".'

If Gielgud was then going through a phase of vocal self-indulgence he did not stay in it for long. 'It must have been awfully hard for him, having developed that propensity, to come off it, but he did, and does when he feels the need to. I suppose that the time when people are best is when everything that they are works *for* them – when even their faults are right in a part.'

The pendulum has now swung to the opposite extreme: the verse in Shakespeare is more likely to be ignored than over-stressed. Not that greater realism necessarily brings greater reality. 'Realism can be as phoney as anything, anyhow, just as phoney as the most rhodomontadey sort of declamation ima-ginable. There's a ham natural as well as a ham fat in the other way.'

Actors in the *Romeo and Juliet* company responded warmly to the unaccustomed realism that Olivier introduced but many of the critics were far more hostile than Herbert Farjeon. 'I felt so badly about the flop I made. I remember the next night going to Bronson Albery, the manager, and saying "I'll resign tonight if you like". I got the most terrible notices. I think there was right and wrong on both sides. People I call the honest critics among one's colleagues were I think impressed with the reality I had got into it, and the relationship reality, the absolute physical reality between Juliet and myself for instance, and my physical relations with everybody on the stage. It was generously, sweetly and lauditorily remarked on by one or two people. I remember Guthrie wrote to me about it and he said "I think the critics were right to fault you for your verse-speaking. It isn't very good, you know". I think I learned a little bit during that. It was so funny because a season at the Old Vic followed fairly hard upon that, at the end of which I was referred to as a Shakespearean actor.'

Some of his finest performances have been in Shakespearean parts. When he played Hamlet at the Old Vic in 1937 he again got into trouble with the verse. 'Mr Olivier does not speak verse badly,' James Agate remonstrated. 'He does not speak it at all.' But his voice, his energy and his exciting way of using his body on stage won high praise. He showed his versatility and his capacity for self-disguise by following Hamlet with Sir Toby Belch. He gave a broad extrovert performance and in his next Old Vic role, Henry V, withdrew ascetically into quiet military virtues. His first Macbeth completed his first year at the Old Vic and then in 1938, as Iago, he used the idea of a homosexual attraction to Othello. His Coriolanus (1938) added considerably to his reputation as an actor in the heroic tradition, but it was not until the 1944 season at the Old Vic, when he first played Richard III, that he became a star of the greatest magnitude. In an interview with Kenneth Tynan he has said 'There is a phrase – the sweet smell of success – and I can only tell you (I've had two experiences of that), it just smells like Brighton and oyster-bars and things like that. And as I went on to the stage – the house was not even full – I felt this thing. I felt a little power of hypnotism; I felt that I had them. It went to my head, as I said, to such an extent that I didn't even bother to put on the limp. I thought, I've got them anyway, I needn't bother with all this characterization any more.' In 1945 at the Vic his famous stammering Hotspur was followed, in *Part Two* of *Henry IV* by a beautifully contrasted study in doddering senility as Shallow. He played Lear in 1946, Antony in 1951, Titus Andronicus and Malvolio at Stratford-on-Avon in 1955, Othello in 1964 and Shylock in 1970.

His versatility outside the Shakespearean canon has been equally admirable. He was the original Stanhope in the Stage Society's production of *Journey's End* and the original Victor in Coward's *Private Lives*. He played Sergius in *Arms and the Man* at the Old Vic and in one famous double bill there he unforgettably doubled Sophocles's Oedipus with Mr Puff in Sheridan's *The Critic*. He played the Duke in Fry's *Venus Observed* and Fred Midway with a Birmingham accent in David Turner's *Semi-Detached*. Without knowing that all three were Laurence Olivier it would have been hard to recognize the same actor in Osborne's Archie Rice, Congreve's Tattle in *Love for Love* and the Jewish lawyer in Somerset Maugham's *Home and Beauty*.

'I don't know if one does understand one's range. One thing

I'm certain of is that it narrows off as one gets older. There's one thing that dictates that and that's the age itself. When you're a useful age, say between thirty and thirty-five, you can still play Romeo, and you can also play King Lear. Your range is that big because those are the sort of things you can do. But when you get to be King Lear's age, how many ways are there that you can do it? Your way of playing a sixty-five, seventy year old man, your field, has narrowed down to that anyway. Yes, you can find different sorts of men of sixty. The doctor I've just done in *Three Sisters* I hope is unrecognizable from the Captain in *The Dance of Death*. But you very seldom get such widely different sorts of people after a certain age.

What about the solicitor in Somerset Maugham?

'That's a bit of pantomime there. You couldn't do that in a very big part, and keep it clear of everything else. That's taking advantage of a minor role in order to make a small creation, which you can just hold watertight for that amount of time, but if that were stretched over a whole evening, they'd be bound to see bits of Archie Rice come into it, and bits of this and bits of that. You know you can't do it. One started one's life fairly gallantly in rep thinking "Nobody's going to recognize me this week from the people who saw me last week". But as you get older, the things you discover become the things which adhere to you. You say "I wish to God I hadn't done that trick of blinking my eyes in the last part I played because it would be so much more useful this week, and much truer to the character than the one I played last week".

'You can see people doing just the same things, using everything they've got. I remember when I was directing Colin Blakeley in Miller's *The Crucible*, which was soon after he'd played Philoctetes, and I kept saying "Colin don't limp". But having limped through a part successfully like that, suddenly it doesn't feel real if you don't do that. It's a refuge. A mannerism is something you develop in order to make you feel more comfortable. And if one day you're terribly nervous on a first night, someone says "The carriage waits, my lord. My Lord Pilkington – " and if one day you come on and go like that (tucking his chin into his shoulder and lumbering one-sidedly) because you're shy of the audience or something – if you don't know it, you're stuck with that for life. Because you

cannot bear the thought of not having one little refuge, something you're used to – a habit – something to make you comfortable. When we go to bed we usually get into the same
position, foetal or not – it's comfort. Therefore when you
come on the stage and you think "Oh God, I hope I don't get
the wind up, Oh God I hope I've got this, Oh God I hope I
remember that", and then you do that (going into the same
position) that's at least home for a minute, a second. Your
anxiety is to feel at home if you're up in an awkward draughty
position like you are on a stage in front of a lot of people –
therefore for John Gielgud a certain tone of voice is home.
You lean on those, find refuge in those things, they're terribly
seductive. So that a thing you've done before feels real because you're used to it – you don't realize that at the time. It's
impossible to go on stretching yourself into being different
shapes and sizes, particularly as your age is governing the main
factor which is stopping you playing Romeo at least. You
don't do that. You can't even play Mercutio. I was a bit old
for the Captain in *The Dance of Death* really. You're supposed
to be fifty. I suppose I'm fairly young for my age. My way
of carrying on is fairly young – I realize that. I've kept very
fit and very physical and all that. But there are a lot of things
that one does with one's body that one does unknowingly in
the search for a refuge.'

A habit that has helped him to develop and sustain his protean
range is his way of concentrating on physical details, whether
of costume or make-up, accent or prop, in the process of
adapting to them. Ronald Pickup, who has spent most of his
career in the National company, has gained a lot from watching Olivier. 'What I've learnt from him is always to deal in
specific very concrete intentions, never in generalizations. You
have to know exactly why you're doing and saying anything at
any moment. That's what creates a faster rhythm. He took such
pains that his watch-strap was right in O'Neill's *Long Day's
Journey*, and he wore his suit for three or four weeks before
we opened. He asked me the other day what sort of walk I'd
got for Richard II. I hadn't actually got a walk at that time
but it made me think about that and about other things
related to it. It's getting a comfortable physical sensation for

the character and knowing that everything about you feels right. Everything then becomes effortless. The intentions take over and you start to fly. What I've learnt about Olivier – which is not the most readily apparent thing – is the dazzling speed at which his thinking happens in terms of the character, this marvellous driving rhythm, the ability to be operating on about eight different levels at once, always keeping an audience on the hop, never letting them get ahead. It really boils down to rhythm. The pulse-beat of anything is what drives it along, and the faster your rhythm is, the more exciting you're likely to be.'

This view of his powers as an actor is confirmed and complemented by Albert Finney's experience of understudying his Coriolanus. 'What one did learn from that is how a great actor can take the kind of peaks and the valleys of a performance, the ups and downs of a character as written and push them even further apart. He makes the climaxes higher, and he makes the depths of it lower, than you feel is possible in the text.'

While John Gielgud keeps his mind alert and derives a good deal of his inspiration from reading and looking at pictures in galleries, Olivier seems to draw more on physical experience. 'I learnt a lot about a very essential factor in acting – poise, the feeling of poise – from flying an aeroplane. It was very interesting, because your two enemies are tautness and ultra-relaxation, in anything you're trying to do, if it's cricket or any physical thing. And acting is largely a physical thing – it's to do with the senses of all sorts. It's the same equation you've got to find between tautness or over-relaxation, or between under-confidence or over-confidence. It's very difficult to find just the right amount. The difficulty of acting, I've always thought, is finding the right humility towards the work and the right confidence to carry it out. With flying you have to learn at least a very exact, precise poise, between your feet being too heavy on the rudder, or your hand too heavy on the stick or too savage on the throttle. You learn a kind of very special poise. And that I've managed to bring into the acting – frightfully useful. Or managed to remember it when I needed to. "Now wait a miute, you're taut". Or "You're too relaxed". It's come in very useful.'

It cannot be said that his relationship with Iago came off

well in the National Theatre *Othello,* but his ideas about it derived partly from wartime experience. 'Rather in common with most people I've come to look on the NCO Iago as the right one, because from my own experience in the war, I've known what an Iago felt like. I've seen people's expressions in the mess or the ward room or whatever you call it, when somebody suddenly gets a half stripe that they'd thought was going to be theirs. I've been conscious of situations in the service myself when with certain groups of men in certain ranks, you find things in yourself that you didn't know were there in the way of jealousies and sensitivities and bloody-mindedness and hatred. And you could be guilty of Iago's offence with the greatest of ease, if you hadn't had just enough sense. I've wanted to kill men, I've wanted to do people down very much when I was in the service, and I think in every service they know that. It's a difficult life. I found the so-called ordinary people so terribly ordinary, so lacking in imagination, I'd hate them for it. They didn't understand each other's feelings at all. I thought when I joined "How marvellous, now I shall know real people, instead of this froth that I've been living amongst all my life". My God, give me the froth every time for real people. Real people are artists. Ordinary people aren't. They just exist in a kind of vacuum. Without any pity, feeling, imagination about each other's troubles or woes or sensitivities or sensibilities. Almost inhuman, I found the real people.'

The frustration Olivier feels at the diminution of range that age brings must have been compensated at least by the satisfactions of directing both in the theatre and the cinema, and of managing, first in the commercial theatre, then at Chichester and the National. His company, Laurence Olivier Productions Limited, presented several plays in the West End, and in 1950, after five years as a Joint Artistic Director of the Old Vic, he leased the St James's Theatre which he kept until 1956, the year before it was closed down. Apart from the plays in which he and his wife Vivien Leigh starred, he presented Dennis Cannan's *Captain Carvallo,* the Orson Welles *Othello* and Tyrone Guthrie's play *Top of the Ladder,* but he also had to sub-let the theatre for long periods. His association with Guthrie, which had begun at the Old Vic, was to culminate in the planning of the Chichester Festival Theatre. Its design was inspired by Guthrie; Olivier was Artistic

Director for its first four seasons; Guthrie had encouraged
Leslie Evershed Martin in the formidable task of raising the
money and bringing the theatre into existence. So Olivier's assumption of the artistic crown when our National Theatre
opened in 1963 was the culmination of a long career in theatrical management. Of course the strain of running a large company as well as acting and directing was enormous. 'The thing
that tires you most and quickest is the thing you resist first.
And of course that's the acting. With all that I've got to do
today and a performance tonight, I think that would make me
feel tomorrow "I don't think I can manage". With *Othello* for
instance, I really felt all the next day I was useless in the office
– as if I had been run over by a bus.'

Olivier's orientation has always been primarily towards the
theatre, but he has also devoted a considerable proportion of
his career to the cinema. He spent 1938-40 in Hollywood and
he has appeared in over forty films, as well as directing six.
His work as a film director has been strongly influenced by the
feeling for rhythm and for shape that he had acquired in the
theatre. His three Shakespeare films, *Henry V*, *Hamlet* and
Richard III undoubtedly won a wider audience for Shakespeare than he had ever had before – even in the cinema – but
Olivier has had to make cuts that he very much regretted. 'I
had to tear my heart out by cutting "All occasions" in *Hamlet*,
which to me is of course the most important speech of the
play. But you have to cut it, because it was just dangerous to
get discursive there, from a film put-together point of view.
Because of the solid impact the medium needs, it has to exist
in a certain form – there are a variety of forms of course. It's
just that certain things are dangerous in certain ways, on certain subjects, in certain conditions, and you probably don't
really know until you see the rushes.' In *Richard III* he had
to cut heavily into Clarence's scene. 'It's a long scene. Nothing's
long, as long as it doesn't seem long but the early part of the
picture seemed a long time getting going. And there are some
points in a film – rhythm of course is the chief of all our
studies – when you just know it's dangerous to get discursive.'

He also had complicated problems of shape and rhythm in
the film he made of Chekhov's *Three Sisters*, though it was an
advantage, of course, to have become so familiar with the play
from directing it in the theatre. 'I've always known the

dangerous moments in it. The danger is the second act of the four. Not the third, which everybody thinks is the dangerous one – the first scene, when everybody is so lazy they can do nothing but sit about. That holds together like a glove.' He was determined to make the film very much more than a cinematic record of his National Theatre production, though he used many of the same actors in the same parts. 'It's a proper film, but you don't go outside and have scenes of people fire-fighting – that's so boring and you can't, there isn't time. Whenever I did get at all discursive, I found that the film people, who were my advisors, and in some sense I suppose my bosses, the Boulting brothers and Sidney Gilliat of British Lion – all they wanted to cut were the bits I put in to make it more like a film, to get out of that room, to create a little scene, down a staircase or in another room. They said "That holds up the action. Get back to it", and I said "Now you're forcing me back onto the stage again". But the only thing I did try to lend myself to was more filmic ideas of setting and getting a little out of the usual way of thinking about that play.'

Though there was a great deal that he liked about Sidney Lumet's film of Chekhov's *The Seagull*, the main influence that it exerted on him was negative. 'It looked marvellous sometimes. There is the occasional pure Monet, for instance, in that shot with Vanessa on the left in full figure, with the lake and rushes behind, looking at him, the first time she fell in love with him. A lot of it was very good. But I was grateful to it because it drove me away from reality for my own film because I thought "You couldn't have had more help from reality, realism, real trees". But I don't actually believe they help Chekhov. All I think you can do is to serve the author rhythmically. And all I said to Josef Svoboda, who designed *Three Sisters*, was "Look, I don't care how you do it, I'm having one interval and I will give you one minute to change from the bedroom (Act Three) to the garden (Act Four), one minute. Now do anything you like". And the change took one minute fifty seconds. That's the thing to do for Chekhov – one interval, no more. By the time they've gone out for their third whisky, they say "What's happened now? Where are we? Did they get to Moscow?" You've let Chekhov kill himself with those three intervals. It's so palpably right to go straight from Act One to Act Two of *Uncle Vanya*, straight from Act Three to Act Four. Because of the rhythm. It was that alone that made the productions perhaps better than they've often been. It made all the difference to the audience's attention and participation. It was simply that they were allowed to stay there. All right you give them half a minute, while they breathe or you play something to make a light change happen or something, and they're still there instead of all this business of "What's this? Did you see . . .?" All that bar-room conversation, it's fatal.'

ARTHUR MILLER

Father-fixation may be one of Arthur Miller's weaknesses as a dramatist but it is also one of his greatest sources of strength. *Death of a Salesman* (1949), his second major play to be produced, is technically a huge advance on the first, *All My Sons* (1948), but mainly because he had found a form which allowed present and past to be interwoven so tightly as to produce a mesh porous enough to absorb all the neurotic energy he produced by opening himself to the theme of love between father and son. In both plays, an ideological conflict cuts against the basic love. In *All My Sons* both the dead son and the survivor felt committed to society in a way the father did not. The tragedy of the two sons in *Death of a Salesman* is that they have to confront almost insane inconsistencies in a once-loved father who is both representative of the society they live in and a victim of the self-alienation its pressures have produced. The theme of betrayal by the father is submerged but unmistakably present in *The Crucible* (1953), but the vicious religiosity of the judge who sentences so many 'witches', male and female, to death, makes him rather like a Puritan patriarch sacrificing a whole tribe of Isaacs, while the love that John Proctor, the hero, feels but refuses to admit towards the young Abigail has something of an incestuous flavour. In the first published text of the play, there is a scene (which was later cut) suggesting that this illicit love triggers off the ensuing catastrophe. In *A View from the Bridge* (1955), the son is again translated into a girl. Eddie Carbone is presented as a hero, but his heroism consists mainly of his refusal to suppress or deny the incestuous passion he feels for his niece. In *After the Fall* (1964), the real father is only one of several father-figures who betray the hero in different ways. In *Incident at Vichy* (also 1964), the aristocrat who initially felt no kinship with the Jew becomes a father-figure by showing himself willing to risk his life to save him from the Nazis. In Miller's most recent play, *The Price* (1968), we are again dealing explicitly with a father and two sons: the main climax is a revelation that there was no real love in the home where the boys grew up. The mother is mentioned only incidentally. And Victor, the policeman-hero, comes to terms with his past only when he acknowledges the genuineness of the love he felt for his selfish old father. As Miller puts it, 'The forces of family and society are laid bare to the point where the man could recognize himself in his actions. When this play starts, he says "I can't find myself in what I've done". Until he discovers that he did love the old man. It's the recrudescence of that feeling, and that explains how he got into this situation, so that his experience becomes his own, rather than some imposed unreality. That is the story structure of the thing.' In this case, though, the father has been dead for sixteen years, and Victor is fighting only with the remnants of the man inside his own consciousness. As Miller says, 'The father's simply there as a shadow. In truth it's related to the other plays in the sense that there are fathers in the other plays and there are sons, but they aren't really struggling with him. Right at the beginning of the play Victor says "I don't know what the hell I was doing here. It was some kind of insanity I had, that I dragged up all his stuff as though it was made of gold, and I sat with this poor fool, who was nothing but one of many bankrupted people, and to me it was as though a mountain had crashed". But if the father has the last laugh, it's a hollow one. It's the end of a force rather than the description of some force in being.'

In spite of the detail Miller includes about Victor's uniform and his having made only nineteen arrests in twenty-eight years, he is less convincing as a policeman than Willy is as a salesman, but it was not an arbitrary decision to make him a policeman. 'The police force does do a hell of a lot to a man. I mean the whole idea of his authoritarianism, the feeling that he's got to be an authority over himself. He doesn't easily accept the fact that he's helpless. Which of course is a fashionable feeling these days. You can't tell the truth about yourself unless you start by saying " Well of course I don't know what I'm doing and I'm helpless ", and if you can't say that, then you can't begin to speak. But Victor won't say that. Because he can't do the job if he says that. He can't believe it, he can't feel that way. He's got to act all the time. He's got to make up his mind twenty-five times a day what to do.'

The incest theme which surfaces in *A View from the Bridge* was recurrent in classical tragedy, and Miller, while writing the play, felt that the story had ancient roots. 'It was as though I was working on something that existed, even though I don't know what literature deals with that particular tale. I've never come across it before or since, but it has a resonance for me of something which had already been written, or if not written, then told. Something in being. I didn't feel I was making anything up.

'The play has been done all over Italy. Raf Vallone toured it three times and played it in places that haven't seen a play in a hundred years. In big opera houses down in Calabria, in Sicily, in places where there's nothing – and the reaction is fantastic. As you know, in Italy, there's no theatre of that sort. It just doesn't happen. But I'm very pleased about the reaction. After all, I'm writing about them from this side of the water, and I can't pretend to know them that well, but they feel it's their show.

'When they staged the play off Broadway – they were playing it for a couple of years downtown – one of the actors told me that an old man used to come every week or two and see the play, kept coming back about half-a-dozen times. He was an old Italian labourer. One of the actors was Italian and talked with him – the guy could barely speak English – and the man was ravished. At the end of the performance he was in tears and would go out sobbing. So the actor asked him why he came back all the time, and he said that that was the story of some relative of his, excepting that the ending was different. And the actor asked him how it had ended in reality, and he said "Well, the girl killed him". And she was sent to prison. Which is marvellous. That's Greek tragedy. But in all the details it was exactly the same – including the submarines, the illegal immigrants, and so forth. That's therefore – so to speak – the ancient root of the story.'

Miller has very seldom worked with stories that pre-existed. Normally it takes him a year to invent a plot and with *All My*

Sons, which is extremely complex, it took two years. It often occurred to him that even Shakespeare might have been a good deal less prolific if he had not been building his plays out of ready-made stories, whether historical or fictional. 'You could telescope characters and make one out of three, and shift and turn and so on, but the basic pattern of the event was there before you, and the *dramatis personae* were there. And I could imagine somebody going on endlessly with historical stories.'

But the only historical play by Miller to be staged was *The Crucible*. 'I once wrote – very early on, when I first started writing – a play about Montezuma and Cortes, which is purely historical. I vaguely recall writing something else on a historical theme long before I started to get plays produced. I never did it after that, except in *The Crucible*.'

But his plays resemble classical, Shakespearean, and historical plays in having a hero. 'To use the word hero today is anathema, because we're most interested in the sinister complications of people, the sinister contradictions which end up as the anti-hero. I still believe, though, that there are people who are heroes in a sense – not because they have heroic values – but somebody may become an exemplar of some sort, somebody who is forced to act in such a way that his action throws light on all the people who remain passive. There are such people. Some of them just murder a lot of other people. I read in the paper this morning the story of a man who killed practically all his relatives yesterday in some place in New Jersey across the river. He'd been a scoutmaster and a ski-instructor. His wife had left him – taken their two children and moved next door with her relatives. He brooded about it long enough and then went in and slaughtered everybody. They tried to gun him down on a highway in the middle of a snow blizzard. The police couldn't see anything. He killed himself finally, shot himself. He'd broken into a store, stolen several rifles and a lot of ammunition and ended up a real outlaw – this man who used to take children on outings and had been a member of the ski-patrol, a volunteer organization to help wounded skiers on hillsides. That's a hero in a sense. The contradictions of the community are in this guy to the point of violence, the point where he explodes. The values that somehow have suddenly collapsed inside him would throw light on the values of all those who have not yet killed anybody. He is representative in that degree.'

Ibsen's habit of bringing social problems into focus through a hero representative of society's contradictions may provide one common factor between his plays and Miller's, but Miller's critics have tended to exaggerate Ibsen's influence on him. He attributes this to an essay he once wrote about Ibsen. 'It's as though I had never written anything else but Ibsenesque plays. They give you back what you gave them. If an author ever writes any kind of essay, they take his statements about something that may be remotely connected with his own work and then interpret it in the light of those statements. Because it's so much easier for them than looking at the work itself and making up their own minds about it.

'But I frankly don't see either Ibsen or Chekhov as being a basis for working now. Probably for extra-dramatic reasons. Ibsen, for example, is regarded in the States as primarily a social playwright. He wrote plays about the water supply or syphilis – "problems" – and that's what they think of him as. But of course that's a small part of his output, and I personally think it's a small, and maybe minor, part of his mind. Ibsen was a mystic, in my view of him. All these characters he's allegedly so carefully building up are really metaphors of various life-forces, death-forces, contradictions and so forth. It's working on a metaphor that's behind the surface reality. And he's interested in heroism and sacrifice. When you read *Brand* or *When We Dead Awaken* or in fact the bulk of his work from the beginning, it's not what we think of at all. The work that shocked the world was *Ghosts*. *A Doll's House*, *An Enemy of the People*, *Pillars of Society*, maybe. These plays show him as a man brought up in a tight little smug community off the sea there, surrounded by fjords, where everybody's eating everybody else, that sort of thing. That's not what I think of at all when I think of Ibsen. The other stuff is basically disregarded – *Brand*, *Rosmersholm*. These are *really* Ibsen.'

What he originally got from Ibsen was 'a sense of the past and a sense of the rootedness of everything that happens'. As Miller says, he is more interested in analysing than in giving an 'impersonation of life'. He is less concerned with reproducing the surfaces of things as they are than with delving into the processes that made them what they are. This implies the kind of involvement with cause and effect which has become very unfashionable. The tendency today, both in the theatre and outside it, is to be very sceptical about diagnoses of causal relationships. The past no longer exists. For Beckett, the man who is enjoying his lunch is no longer the same person as the man who was looking forward to it. This makes it virtually impossible to draw an outline round a character, whereas Miller's whole sense of the reality of a character depends on acknowledging the limits surrounding it. In his 1958 Introduction to his *Collected Plays*, he explained that for him it was essential 'not only to depict why a man does what he does or why he nearly didn't do it, but why he cannot simply walk away and say to hell with it . . . I take it that if one could know enough about any human being, one could discover some conflict, some value, some challenge, however minor or major, which he cannot find it in himself to walk away from.'

One of the reasons his early plays have tragic endings is that the heroes are being tested by society in such a way that it is only by dying that they can show what it is they are unable to walk away from. Because he fails as a salesman, Willy Loman can no longer be a useful member of the materialistic society to which he has committed his entire existence. In *The Crucible*, John Proctor dies rather than let his name be used to support the unjust lawcourt that is mass-producing death sentences for his fellow-citizens; in *A View from the Bridge*, Eddie Carbone refuses to walk away from the course of action to which his undeniable passion for his niece commits him. *The Price* is more of a comedy, in that more of the action and dialogue are comic, and the ultimate violence is avoided. Victor, as a policeman, is too self-disciplined to be a tragic hero. For the play this is an advantage. For the character, as Miller says, 'it's also a limitation in my own sense of the reality in this kind of a man. He couldn't have done what he did, with the discipline with which he did it, and then suddenly break with the whole character that he's got.' But Miller is well aware that this view of character is unfashionable. 'This is unacceptable today. It implies that people have limits. What we're confronted with all the time in the theatre today is somebody suddenly doing something which is absolutely inexplicable by any standards, just for the theatrical effect. Because here is where he is supposed to break down. I don't want to do that.'

Miller's concept of character is totally different from Beckett's, for instance. 'You made a point in your book on Beckett – the quality of monologue in the dialogue has always struck me. That is to say that you can change the names a great many times – not always – as to who is speaking. Because it's basically a man talking to himself – namely the creator of this work. Which all plays are. It's inconceivable to create characters excepting as a projection of the author.' But Miller, unlike Beckett, is a playwright who depends to a considerable extent on having a good ear for variations of syntax and accent, and on his ability to reproduce them in his dialogue. As he says, speech patterns and dialects are deeply connected with attitudes, especially in a country like the United States where such a large proportion of the population consists of immigrants. 'A man who's from a family that's been in America for two hundred years is one kettle of fish, and somebody who's a first generation immigrant, who's wearing the same clothes as the other fellow and may even have the same education – I can detect where the parting of the ways came, and a certain defensiveness or aggressiveness may be expressed by one man in his speech and not by the other fellow, because he no longer needs to be aggressive. He's got it. He's part of the realm, so to speak. I suppose you have it in England too, but it's not quite the same.'

Not that Miller is laboriously naturalistic in his mimicry. The dialogue of characters like Solomon, the old Jewish antique dealer in *The Price*, is idiomatic and idiosyncratic, but it is also highly compressed. Working on his earlier plays, Miller often wrote one draft in verse in order to tighten the dialogue and heighten his own awareness of the characters' rhythms before rewriting in prose. Normally he would not want his audience to have any awareness of listening to something that had been conceived as verse, but in the one-act version of *A View from the Bridge* (1955) a good deal of verse still remains – mainly in the choric monologues of the lawyer, Alfieri. But in most of his plays, all that remains is the economy. 'The compression has a reason for it, aside from the fact that I like that kind of speech anyway: it's more interesting than to distend something. The thing that I find so discouraging in the theatre so much of the time is the length of time it takes to say the most apallingly obvious thing. Even in some work that is seriously intended. It's as though there's a certain weak-mindedness – as though nobody could handle two ideas at the same time. I think that they have falsely interpreted Beckett in that respect, because to the naked eye he seems to be doing just that in his one-line and two-line speeches. Somebody says "What time is it?" But in the context it's immensely complicated. The playwrights who copy him have avoided the complications – they simply ask you what time is it in thirty-five different ways and it gets pretty tearing after a while. It advances you backwards into the kindergarten. I think life is much more interesting than that, and art ought to be more interesting than life. I can hear better conversations on Sixth Avenue and Fifty-Fifth Street from that viewpoint.'

If Beckett and Brecht are the two strongest prevailing currents in our theatre, Miller, though he greatly admires both writers, has great reservations about the directions in which they are carrying us. Even when it was first produced in Germany during the twenties, Brecht's work never had the effect it was intended to have. 'I don't know enough about what the conditions of production have been, but from what I can piece together, he's never been successful excepting with middle-class audiences. Do you know of situations where he found the audience he was after, the working-class audience? So what then happens to his theory, which was based on the idea that the worker has to be educated to be alienated from the society he's in?'

Has Brecht had any influence on you?

'Not really, because I've never finally believed in this attempt to separate man into a thinking analytical beast on the one hand and a feeling one on the other – which is what the Alienation Effect finally comes down to, in operation. In other words, the emotions are only to be stated, so that we're never swept up in them. It doesn't work in his plays. You are swept up by them, maybe even more so because they are underplayed or separated from the actor in a certain way. Therefore I feel that since the emotions do come out anyway, why not use them? Also I don't think man is – or should be – that rational in the sense that he sees so much more than he feels. The ideas we live by are the ones that we feel the most, and instead of disintegrating I want to integrate them. I do think society is disintegrating them, and why should I collaborate in that? I think there is already too much alienation for the survival of the human being. It doesn't necessarily give insight. It simply gives resignation, acidity, cynicism, nihilism, in my observation. The people who helped me in my life when I was in trouble were integrated people, strangers who could be moved by a person to the point where even against their own interests they would go out of their way to be of use. Because of some virtuous ideal, perhaps, or because of a sense of themselves and what they want. And I don't think you're going to make either a revolution or a better world with disintegrated people, people who are alienated to that degree, with no relation between what they think and what they feel. Because the easiest thing you can do is to rationalize yourself into false positions of heroism or false positions of negation, cynicism and passivity.'

Nor has Miller a high regard for the work of the younger playwrights, labouring under the shadow of Beckett and Ionesco. 'They never *finish* anything. I think they mistakenly associate any kind of aesthetic finish with authoritarianism. The attitude being "You make out of it what you wish". This whole obfuscation business is carried to the point where they simply don't any longer take seriously the idea that the author should have an intention, let alone any coherent intention, however mysterious it might be. It should simply be an effusive attempt to express some vague feeling.

'There's a terrible fraud going on, I think. Awful conformism. I went to Yale in 1967 just for an evening and I talked to about a dozen students who were interested in writing. And at a certain point in the conversation I asked what sort of things they were writing. First one boy described his work, then another, and they were all writing versions of either *Rhinoceros* or *Endgame* or something of this kind. I said to one boy "In other words it's pretty much of a uniform style". And one boy said "Yeah, well, it's easier that way". He said "You could do it in a morning". However, the fact that you could do it in a morning was not quite a source of cynicism to him. It was almost a sign that there was some virtue of sincerity in the work. Because if you have to think twice about something, it means that there's a tactic involved. It's like imagining that blurting out something is always truer than considering it. It's the virtue of inner-directedness. I said to them that it was amazing that when I was starting out people were writing verse dramas, all kinds of dramas. There was even a little fad for Japanese Noh dramas. Not that we weren't as conformist as anybody else, but it took different forms. Now it's totally dominated by *one* form. And the terrible thing was to hear that some of these kids came from Texas or Oklahoma, or Michigan, from all over the United States. And they're all writing the same thing. It's quite a comment, I thought. They're totally unrelated kids, except that they happen to be in the same school.'

Miller has a limited belief in the usefulness of playwriting courses. His own experience of one in Michigan was valuable at least in that it gave him the chance to see his plays being performed in front of an audience consisting of the other students, at a time when there were no outlets for a playwright's work except in the commercial theatre. 'Even then we knew it was dying. Nevertheless it had more productions than there are today. I suppose there must have been twenty-five serious plays a year of which one or two were worth looking at. But there was still a tradition of doing "serious" plays. And you couldn't produce a one-act play on Broadway at all. And indeed it's still not easy, even now. But there are plenty of outlets in Off-Broadway and Off-Off-Broadway. A kid today writes ten pages and a group or a gang will do it.'

He maintains, however, that there is a sense in which playwriting can be taught. 'It's a conventional form, no matter how unconventional it appears – conventional in the sense that there is an audience, there are actors, there are limitations to those actors, and so forth. So at least what could come of the teaching, if it's well done, is awareness of the rudimentary nature of the medium. It makes them more acutely aware of what's gone before, what the form is. But of course you can't make a playwright out of someone without the talent for it – any more than you make writers out of teaching versification or something, though the study of prosody might give him some insight into writing which he might never otherwise have. It's all very doubtful. But in that class they used to manage to go on into other fields. It's a good starting point to talk about all sorts of things – physics, chemistry and stuff. So there is, I suppose, some education there, but I wouldn't say it would make a playwright out of him.

'A play is essentially a mechanism for communicating, and all the techniques involved must be related to that. It involves an audience. That is to say a play can't take six hours. A novel can go on for ever. There's also a minimum time limit – a play lasting for three minutes is not likely to register very much. It has to be of a certain magnitude. Of course that magnitude now has been shifted and changed beyond recognition. I mean nobody knows the difference any more between an anecdote and a play. If it's an anecdote, it's good. In fact, if it's narrative anecdote and it's not even dramatic, it passes. I'm not sure it's a bad thing to go through, but it's a cul-de-sac if one imagines that this is the object of it.'

Although he does not try to think, while writing, of the size of the audience he is trying to reach, Miller cannot totally exclude some awareness of it, and when writing a screenplay like *The Misfits* (1961), he found himself simplifying much more than he would in a stage play, partly because of size of potential audience, partly because the visual element is so much more dominant in a film. 'I suppose it's the fact that what you see is much more commonplace than what you hear, and it's inevitably going to be that way, perhaps because we learn how to speak much later than we learn how to see. The infant a month old is already learning to discern one person from another, one emotion on a face from another emotion and one sound from another, to a degree that it means something. Loud sounds, soft ones, pleasant ones. But words refer not only to emotions but ideas, concepts and so forth that are difficult to define. So that the whole thing becomes much more intriguing and subtle.

'The difficulty of arriving at a satisfactory theatrical form in the present cultural situation may be connected with this. There's no ready standard for the application of words, as there used to be. But with images, the mere fact that the camera shoots something gives it an existence, but the mere fact that somebody says something proves nothing or only proves that he said it.

'The prevailing artistic modes are both the result and the cause of prevailing habits of expression. People find the form for their feelings in art so much that they're not even aware of it. They're doing what the art tells them is real and right or stylish or relevant or apt to do. In a different time it's a different kind of a character maybe. It's just like insanity. People of different ages take on different types of psychosis. They become popular. And this must be a social thing. After all, by what incredible statistical option do most people who are sick today become hysterics? At another time they would have become something else, perhaps manic-depressive psychotics. It has to be something in a particular society that ordains a particular illness. So much of this lacks ultimate reality to me, because I can see in so many cases the taking on of a social attitude. It may not express anything really profound in the person at all: it merely expresses the way he acclimatizes himself to his moment.'

This consciousness of the effect that art has on fashion cannot be taken as evidence that Miller, as a practising artist, is consciously trying to influence his audience, or even believes that he could. 'I doubt very much that works of art – excepting in a rare situation – have a direct effect on audience behaviour outside the theatre. It's indirect – I think that they do derive from works of art certain basic concepts about how one is supposed to behave, what attitudes one is supposed to have. But, finally, life is more powerful. I don't think art is finally decisive in that, though it's got a lot to do with it. The best I can hope for is that people will see better in a general sense, and – more than anything else – that they will not give up.

'I find that each of my plays is based on some conception of the value of life. I don't believe in plays that give us the portentous news that life is over. I don't think the writer really believes that anyway. The act of communication is an act of help. I don't care how perverse the material is. Total pessimism is only possible for somebody who just goes silent, and once he speaks it's a contradiction of the basis.'

At the same time, Miller is acutely aware of the strength of the self-destructive force operating in our society. 'Without it I couldn't have written any of the plays that I've written, but I really do believe and always have that we are being encouraged towards self-destruction by one or another of the things we believe about ourselves and about life, about what we should do next and so forth. We make choices on the side of death all the time. It's one of the values in the whole contemporary movement in the theatre which I like very much, that even though the means, very often, are self-indulgent, sloppy and, I think, finally flippant and frivolous, what they're after is life. But you have to be very careful with life, it's very tricky. If you aren't careful enough, you can be digging your own grave and celebrating sunlight at the same time. A little more brains is necessary. Intellectuality is required sometimes, just to think your way through these feelings. And it's appalling how specious that is in so many people. It's ironical too that they're that way when they worship Brecht and Beckett, who spent so much of their time theorizing, thinking, intellectualizing and so forth about what they're doing. And these kids, some of them – most of them that I have any knowledge of – have no use for that.

'And there's another paradox. So much of the intellectualism that has happened is inside naturalism. It's a most paradoxical kind of naturalism because it's only poetic in relation to the most blatantly pedestrian playwriting, which deals with ashtrays, telephones, couches, windows that open and shut and ceilings and effects. But it's an attempt really to take the core of experience, and yet it's called anti-naturalistic. And it's *most* naturalistic. That's one of its failures. The original naturalist – let's say a guy like Zola – conceived of naturalism as delivering up the social organization of the time as well as surface details. That is, he was going to trace out the forces that oppressed the characters, but in the process he was going to put on the stage every detail of real existence. Now the forces themselves have evaporated. The old class struggle, the Marxist idea, has been shot full of holes – man is more contradictory than that – and consequently that side of naturalism, this pure physical representational quality, is out. But if you really recorded the dialogue of two housewives sitting on a subway, you'd have the best kind of contemporary work, and it would be regarded as anti-naturalistic – all the incompleted ideas, the contradictory phrases, the elegancies of speech that are used by inelegant people. I'm not knocking it. I don't think it's good, bad or indifferent. It's just a terribly limited thing.

'You want finally an inner organization that can come to some climax, and some understanding. I suspect that we're not going back to something, but that a new synthesis will finally appear. Because I think that we'll finally get bored with it. It all tends to be very predictable. We know now that nothing's really going to happen, that everything's going to turn sour. That the perverse is going to win, and so forth. Nothing's true if it isn't perverse. But suddenly somebody is going to discover something that is not perverse and is true. And then we'll be off again with a new conception.

'But the idea of synthesizing is out of fashion. They regard that as an artificial implantation. I couldn't work that way. It's like action painters throwing paint on the canvas. There's no synthesis there, it's simply raw material. You need science to do the synthesizing. It's a kind of Luddite idea. Intellectuals are always revolting against progress. They always have been. Even when they call for it. When it happens, they hate it. From the invention of the railroad to everything else. They're arch-conservatives, always – great looking-backers. It's something like that that's going on now. Science is so practical, and the reaction is against it. Everything you touch turns to a jail, a prison, a new kind of implantation of the unnatural. Just as it did to Thoreau, to Emerson, to Henry James – to a whole host of American writers. They were all in mourning for the past, in one way or another. Natural man against a synthesis which puts him in a false position. And now we're again with the natural man. The difference is that we take a Greek tragedy and turn it into a physical threat to the audience. This is truer because it's tactile, it's unintellectual. It has nothing to do with conceptions and so forth. It's Rousseau, all over again. It's the mind at the end of its tether. So what's left? The body, and the senses. And the idea of synthesizing what one can perceive with what one feels is not on the cards at the moment.'

That an unfashionable play like *The Price* can run for over a year on Broadway obviously proves that there is still a need for this sort of drama. Certainly audiences are less hostile to it than critics. 'In America there are perhaps one, or two, critics who are at all sympathetic to what I do or have done. It would be hard to find two. I can think of only one, to tell the truth. I'm assuming that there is somebody, someplace, that I don't know about. I still believe, from my own observation outside the theatre, that the changes in people which are celebrated among us are important. But certain fundamental biological facts remain – there is such a thing as the need to find some usable past, to deal with the past. I don't know a human being who is not obsessed with this, in one way or another. We age. No Absurd drama is going to destroy that, or reverse it. Energy flags. Sheer sensation gets duller instead of sharper once you get past adolescence. The needs of one's children, for justice, for attention, for sacrifice – all these things are as old as man. And those elemental things are what go into my plays. So the audience is still there because those things are still there. They're not going to go away because somebody decides that this is no longer worth talking about. This is the main thing and will always be the main thing. So that's what's left and that's what's there.

'If all one has to do is make noises, then all noises are equally sacred. Then hell, the whole idea of an art, it's all over. And all you can do is replace writer A with writer B, who is not as tired as writer A, and this is exactly what's happened. The writer is getting more and more obsolescent. In fact, there are more and more productions with no writers. Since there is no really underlying conception to anything – well actors do that better than anybody. Put actors on the stage and you have a performance. But an improvisation is an improvisation. It's the difference between playing listlessly on a keyboard and making arbitrary loud noises, and playing some composed structure. This opposition to structure is, I think, the ultimate escape from existence, and I see no sign at the moment that that will reverse itself. Critics simply jump on this wagon and ride it. It's great fun – they don't have to think any more either. There's no discernment necessary. It's just "Were you interested or weren't you? Was it all terribly boring or medium boring?"

'What they call statement now is simply something that is opposed to the Vietnam war, for example. This is supposed to make something relevant when it does nothing of the sort. In other words these are tags. The war is a tag, so that's good for now. When the war ends we have to find another tag, and that's what's supposed to give it relevancy to the human condition. The last time I saw anything like this was in the worst part of the thirties, when everything had to evoke some image of the working class and the class struggle. So out of the window went most of the good stuff that was written in the thirties. And the stuff that seemed so relevant nobody can even find now, except in the most arcane kind of library. It's the same today – they're confusing journalism with the theatre.'

PETER COOK and DUDLEY MOORE

The word *revue* was hardly ever used in the sixties: *Beyond the Fringe* was usually regarded as the show which finished it off and started the vogue for satire. But *satire* has become a very vague term, and in fact, *Beyond the Fringe* was not really a satirical review.

PETER COOK: I don't think any of us set out with any intention of saying 'Let's do a revue which breaks all conventions'. We really sat down to write something which we thought was funny and enjoyed performing, and it hit at a certain point in time which was absolutely right for it, and it did get this rather false reputation of savage satire. One of the things I most enjoyed doing in the show was the miner who wanted to be a judge but didn't have the Latin. Now you could say there was satire in that. He said 'The trouble with being a miner is that when you're too old and weak and stupid to do your job you get the sack. The very opposite applies with judges.' But it was part of a fantasy sketch really.

DUDLEY MOORE: Satire seems to be such a constricting term. When I hear the word I interpret it as a little pocket of political humour, which, in fact, *Beyond the Fringe* wasn't.

P.C.: On the whole satire is better done in magazine form — says he, plugging *Private Eye*. I was doing *Beyond the Fringe* in America when *That Was The Week That Was* was on television here, but I have a feeling that were they to re-run those shows, they wouldn't hold up that well.

D.M.: Like yesterday's papers.

P.C.: I saw about three of them because I asked to see them, just to see what all this sensation was about, and obviously there were good things in them. Particularly the contributions made by Tim Birdsall,* which I think were the most original. But the simple business of getting up and impersonating politicians I don't think is funny any more.

D.M.: I like it when, say, Mike Yarwood does it, because he does it so well. Maybe one *could* do political satire again. For a start, I don't have any knowledge of politics.

P.C.: (*elderly Scots voice*) But the political figures have become less colourful than they were in the sixties – Mr Victor Feather and Harold Wilson and Ted Heath. (*Normal voice*) They're not ideal figures to parody.

D.M.: One is so inundated on television with all sorts of political dissensions that you can't actually extract figures who are really right for it. Maybe Enoch Powell is – it would be difficult to parody him.

P.C.: (*Powell voice*) Are we to see this country overwhelmed by a tide of Alien People with Alien Ways? – I think he's a figure you could do, but not one I'd choose to do.

D.M.: They've almost become entertainers themselves. He did a thing with Robin Day where he was saying things like (*Frankie Howerd voice*) 'Ooh-oh-ah, did I say that?' It was extraordinary, actually – they're deflecting the possibility of being satirized. It seems almost over-ripe now. As if one is absolutely covered from head to foot with information and so forth and actually to get through all that would be a much more difficult thing.

P.C.: I'm planning to do Amin in *Behind the Fridge*. Not as an impersonation of him – you can scarcely outdo the man himself – but I'd like to do an interview with me as Amin and Dudley just talking to me. (*As Amin*) Because I'm very fond of that type of voice.

D.M.: (*Asian*) And you do it with a lot of relish, man.

P.C.: Oh these Asian buggers, they're movin' about the place, seizin' the economy – So you could call that political, but it's in the realms of lunacy, where he is himself.

D.M.: But there wasn't in fact that much anti-establishment

* The cartoonist and illustrator.

stuff in *Beyond the Fringe*. Peter did a take-off of Macmillan which wasn't so much a Yarwood-type impersonation, as his *impression*. I think we all tended to want to kick against obvious pomposity – which I suppose is what all humour is about.

P.C.: But a lot of the best stuff in it – say the Shakespearean parody – was nothing to do with establishment or non-establishment. It was just knockabout fun.

D.M.: A lot of the sketches probably touched establishment-type things. Alan Bennett's sermon was an upper-class priest who could have come straight out of Magdalen Chapel.

P.C.: If you look round the country today, what sacred cows are there left to knock? I was expecting a question from one interviewer, which indeed I did get: 'Well, what sacred cows will be your targets in your new show *Behind the Fridge?*' And I think there isn't a single sacred cow left. Probably the last of them was Sir Francis Chichester. An attack on Sir Francis Chichester might still be regarded as outrageous. He was a hero. In the reporting of his collision in mid-Atlantic the headline was 'Sir Francis is all right and is on his way back'. And somehow, as a sort of footnote, it was added that three people died in the rescue attempt. I would have said that he was a sacred cow, but I can't think of any others. I suppose cancer is a sacred cow. The very word. I remember Lennie Bruce at the Establishment just using the word 'cancer' and that was it. Somebody in the audience said 'All right, Tricia, Catherine. Out. Cancer. You've heard it. Come on. Let's leave. Cancer. That's it'. And stormed out. And Lennie was just making the point that there are certain words which evoke such a strong reaction – a *gut* reaction – in people that you can't use them, and so you pretend that the whole subject just doesn't exist. I'm not saying that there's an enormous amount of comedy to be got out of cancer, but it's still thought to be hilariously funny if somebody's deaf or blind.

D.M.: Wasn't it W. C. Fields who did a sketch about a blind man? In some early films, blindness was really ridiculed, by people walking through shop windows and things like that. Although the blind themselves would probably find it amusing if they heard about it. (*Dud voice*) Not that they'd be able to see the film, eh?

Peter Cook established his comedy style while at Cambridge, writing sketches which he performed at Footlights 'smokers'. Many of these sketches later found their way to the West End, where they were made into material for Michael Codron's revues *Pieces of Eight* (1959) and *One Over the Eight* (1961), both with Kenneth Williams.

P.C.: There were a lot of sketches in *Pieces of Eight* and *One Over the Eight* which would have been perfectly apt in *Beyond the Fringe*, and vice versa. Which again brings me back to this slight myth about *Beyond the Fringe* – that it had destroyed revue, though at one time it was said to revitalize it! Whereupon there wasn't another revue for about four years. In fact one of my favourite sketches of all time was 'One leg too few'. It was about this one-legged man applying for the part of Tarzan. That couldn't be in *Beyond the Fringe* in the West End because it had been in *Pieces of Eight*. But it was in *Beyond the Fringe* in New York and it didn't seem out of place in the least.

D.M.: In fact there were very, very lightweight areas in *Beyond the Fringe*, although the overall quality was more velvety than was thought normal in revue. Which was much more tinselly, and generally weakened by birds in macintoshes singing songs under lamp-posts and odd dance routines.

P.C.: And those awful point numbers. I really can't stand those. Rather flabby music and slightly smutty lyrics.

D.M.: I remember writing them up at Oxford during early revue days. They all had that sort of (*Sings:*) 'Here we are, eight-thirty again, da-da-da- de-diddle-de-dee.' It was great fun in many ways, but one was in a terrible groove with it.

Peter Cook and Dudley Moore first met in 1959.

P.C.: Brought together by someone called John Bassett, who

was working at the Edinburgh Festival and looking for late-night revue. They'd had Flanders and Swann the year before. And he knew Dudley personally, he knew Jonathan, he'd heard of me.

D.M.: In fact he asked Jonathan and myself to suggest two other people – me one from Oxford and Jonathan one from Cambridge. And Jonathan suggested you. We were very suspicious of each other.

P.C.: I thought Dudley was an ideal person in those days, since he was nicely subservient, humble, kind.

D.M.: Ah, but you're being very naïve here, Peter. Which I'm afraid you have been for the last thirty years and probably for the last twenty-odd before that.

P.C. I realized it masked an inner –

D.M.: You know, I was much more aggressive in those days – and we could get on to astrology here, because this is a typical Scorpio reaction to an Aries. Much more aggressive. Because I've now got a lot of it out. What bothers you is that I've now become a person.

P.C.: A well-rounded human being.

D.M.: Less rounded than I was. Two stone heavier I was in those days. In fact I think we all were. Except Jonathan and Alan, who've been –

P.C.: Consistent.

D.M.: Maybe we didn't meet them in *Beyond the Fringe*.

P.C.: (*toothless don voice*) No, met them in the Terrazza three minutes ago. Awfully charming people. Jonathan's a doctor you know, and he's writing this book on Mesmerism and he's directing Charlton Heston in Los Angeles.

All four have gone on working in show business but Jonathan Miller does not want to do any more performing and Alan Bennett does less than Peter Cook and Dudley Moore. Whereas both Alan Bennett and Jonathan Miller still sound like men who have had an Oxbridge education, the voices of both Peter Cook and Dudley Moore have become protean and almost classless. In fact Peter Cook's cultivation of vocal flexibility may have been inspired partly by an anxiety to escape from a class background he disliked.

P.C.: I was born in Torquay, the Riviera of the English coast, at St Chad's private nursing home. When I was at Cambridge my voice began to lose its Radleigh upper-class tones: the twang went a bit. Because I found my own upper-class voice rather embarrassing.

D.M.: I was born in Charing Cross hospital. I lived in Dagenham from the age of about four. I think we lived somewhere else first, like Wanstead or Leytonstone. When I went to Oxford I couldn't open my mouth when I first got there because (*smooth voice*) everybody was terribly smooth and I really couldn't say a word. And I used to sound like a right fart, because I was trying to sort of 'do the same thing' and it was grotesque. I *did* find my voice very embarrassing because I felt that everybody would be contemptuous of it. In fact, people didn't notice it that much – but I was very aggressive about it. Actually, I go into character voices much less now than I ever did. (*Going into one*) It's the real essence of me coming out as a person, you know, over the years, maturing, you see – Yes, there goes the first voice. I don't know what my voice is – There it is, that was my voice. I used to be told off for saying 'tarl' instead of 'towel'. I suppose it's any performer's natural fear of not having his own voice accepted.

The quartet broke up after the long Broadway run of *Beyond the Fringe* (669 performances), and the partnership between Peter Cook and Dudley Moore began in 1965 with the first of the four television series they have done together. This is when the characters Pete and Dud were born. There was one Pete-and-Dud sketch in *Behind the Fridge* but it is hard to gauge how much the characters have changed over eight years.

D.M.: I think actually the danger is of them becoming too intelligent, too well read. I think at one stage their reactions to things weren't quite so primitively funny as they had been at the beginning. (*BBC voice*) Or would you not agree there?

P.C.: (*Pete voice*) Pete has always been very well educated. Three pages of *Readers' Digest*

D.M.: (*Dud voice*) I think the danger has been that Dud has been contributing too much. He's been reading the odd –

P.C.: Word.

D.M.: – the odd word here and there. And Pete developed a certain line of sarcasm that was detrimental to the relationship. Mind you, Pete and Dud, like any two normal human beings living together, had to go through a certain *crise de coeur*.

P.C.: It took them two years to move. In the first two series they always sat there, and then a great breakthrough came in the third series and they actually got up and walked.

D.M.: In the stage show there was quite a lot of bustling about. Mainly by Dud, who's become quite a virtuoso in the moving. You, of course, remained largely seated. Not through lack of potentiality in the moving area but through sheer laziness. The staging somehow developed into this extraordinary business of Pete sitting on his bottom and me doing all the work.

In fact they both have to work harder in the Pete and Dud sketches than in any of the others.

D.M.: They might be pleased to see us as Pete and Dud, but if after half a minute things haven't gone too well in a sketch, you'll know it. It doesn't matter whether you're Laurel and Hardy or whoever, if it's not working, it's not working. You have to work at keeping the pace and keeping the energy up. I'm quite exhausted when I've done that sketch. Maybe because there's such a lot at stake with those two characters, and it's a shame if it doesn't work because people might feel doubly let down. But when they work, they really do work, and when they don't they're as boring as anything else when it doesn't come off.

They create their own material, sometimes by improvising together into a tape-recorder, sometimes sitting down separately to write.

D.M.: We used to work almost exclusively with a tape-recorder. And then write it, rehearse it and learn it at the same time. We used to take headings down and then say 'We need maybe to reverse this bit and that bit, put another bit in there, and then do it again'. And by a process of elimination and addition we'd come to the final thing. More recently, things have gone straight onto paper – which I personally find more difficult – but sometimes it's useful when one is blocked. It's good to have something facing you on a bit of paper. Although I feel that that's harder to change than when you improvise freshly into a tape-recorder each time. It's a mixture of the two things, really.

P.C.: Even if something is written down, it's altered by doing it into a tape-recorder. We don't just read it – we ad lib from what we've written down. So either way it gets changed.

D.M.: Although the change is slightly different. I think it's harder to become more colloquial from a written script than by keeping it natural with continual improvisation. That's the only drawback.

Inevitably a great deal of material gets wasted.

D.M.: I look back at lots of ideas and I think 'What on earth was that about? It doesn't sound very funny'.

P.C.: On the other hand we've had sketches or ideas for sketches lying around for years, which will suddenly click and you'll see how they work. There's one particular one – a very simple situation of an actor who is doing some domestic work while he is resting. We just thought that was a good situation. I've not actually done domestic work myself, but I've had actors doing it for me, and on the whole it's been remarkable how little domestic work has been done and how much talk about the general state of the theatre, ducky. So that was just a premise, and then suddenly it clicked about a month before we went to Australia, and then developed in rehearsal and in performance over there.

D.M.: What's amazing to me is that certain parts of the sketch that you feel are difficult and not working – suddenly they'll burst into flames and be the high point of the sketch. That's the incredible thing about performing, I suppose. One area of the sketch was a bit wooden. It should have been the high point and it didn't work, and then suddenly we found a tone for it and it just sort of went berserk – marvellous.

P.C.: A lot depends on the rapport between Dudley and me on

the stage. Once one stops listening and really working at
the situation, the whole thing falls flat. Prior to going to
Australia with *Behind the Fridge* I hadn't been on the stage
since 1964 – and I was a bit terrified, but the good things
about it came flooding back so quickly.

D.M.: The marvellous thing is when you get that feedback
and the laughter spirals up. That's the real reward. I'd done
a stage show for nine months – *Play It Again, Sam* – and
then I did a jazz tour in Australia, which was like doing a
stage performance, because it was a whole series of concerts,
which I'd never done before and which I enjoyed. When we
started the tour of *Behind the Fridge* a whole sketch, which
should have been the highpoint of the show from the start,
wasn't at all. It came at the end of the show and then we
moved it to the beginning of the second half and it suddenly
took off and got in the right sort of perspective. My attitude
in the sketch was wrong until suddenly I found what it
should have been, and it went fantastically, after going quite
drably. Conversely, of course, you can get a marvellous
climactic point in a sketch and then suddenly one night you
lose it and you think 'How the hell have I lost it?' It will
take a long time before you get it back again, if ever. That's
strange too. Although it's normally just one line, I find, or
one little bit, that suddenly doesn't work. Then of course
one approaches it with trepidation, every night thinking
'Well I'll get it this time, I'll really work at it tonight', and
it goes wrong, and it's very disconcerting. I remember us
laughing on stage, actually, because there was one line that
used to go like a bomb – it was marvellous – and then
suddenly we couldn't get it. And we used to approach this
line –

P.C.: And start giggling.

D.M.: Because we knew it was going to go wrongly and of
course nobody else knew. There was this mysterious snigger
on stage – which we controlled magnificently, of course,
being pros.

Some of their sketches start from the idea of a character for which a situation has to be devised; sometimes the starting point is a place or a situation.

D.M.: There are certain situations in life that you use, and if you like, exorcise from yourself by doing them on stage. One often acts out on stage situations that were frightening when one was younger or even now. Although I don't think it's a therapeutic thing, eventually.

R.H.: You don't?

D.M.: Well actually, now I come to think of it, I do. When it goes well one is left with a tremendous feeling of satisfaction – perhaps even self-satisfaction. When I came back from Australia I didn't want to perform at al'. Because I'd seen on and off over the years *why* I wanted to perform. I suddenly thought 'No, I don't want to perform any more because I'm obscuring myself, as it were'. But then I realized that there wasn't anything else that I wanted to do. And I do enjoy it very much. So I got over that particularly huge reaction. The way I perform, or the way I contribute material is a way of saying or doing things that I've wanted to do in life but couldn't. My father died a year and a half ago and one way of getting it into some sort of perspective was the idea of doing a sketch about death. I don't say I do that to make myself feel better, but one had such an extraordinary experience there that it maybe sparked things off. I'm sure that personal things are the richest source of material.

P.C.: A lot of my material comes from some inner fantasy which I don't understand. Like the miner who wanted to be a judge. I've never met anybody like that and it wasn't copied. I didn't suddenly meet some schizophrenic and say 'I must do something like that'. So it was obviously something in me which comes out in this form. And I get into that voice, and I'm in that hat with that macintosh, then I become that character. So that's obviously part of me.

D.M.: It's marvellously like someone who's saying, 'I'm not allowed to be myself, you know'. When he's saying 'Oh, I could have been a judge but I didn't have the Latin', it's almost a rationalization of this in character form. I could have said 'Well, I would have wanted to be a concert pianist', and maybe I could do a sketch that relieved that tension, in a way. I think at one time I did worry about getting things done. But now I just hope that I'll do things I enjoy and enjoy them even more.

P.C.: Like the total destruction of all tax records.

D.M.: I used to promise myself that I'd write an opera and things like that, but I don't have any ambitions that way now. Although I'm not sure that there isn't a huge ambition underneath it (*American accent*) which I'm just denying, doctor. But of course it'll take time. It'll come out of its own accord. Well, I think we'll have to stop now. See you next week.

P.C.: (*Harley Street voice*) Mr Moore, you're now seventy-six years old. This opera which you've been talking to me on the couch about for the last – what was it? – fifty-five years – how's it coming along?

D.M.: (*asthmatic septuagenarian*) Well, I've reshaped the opening recitative.

P.C.: That's very good indeed.

D.M.: But I haven't done nothing else. I done the first chord and the last chord of the overture. But what goes in between I don't have any idea.

P.C.: I'm sure it will come to you.

D.M.: Yes.

P.C.: I'm talking about death.

D.M.: I think as you perform you realize somehow you've got to push something a bit more because you're throwing it away, or else you've got to press on with some lines rather than wait for a laugh. Or else you have to take the risk and wait for a laugh and then go on. I think we have a fairly instinctive way of performing, and then it's a matter of feedback with the audience. You adjust to how they react. And you generally find a way of doing it that seems to suit the sketch. Some of the sketches are very broad, very grotesque, camp, theatrical. And it's amazing the sort of reaction you can get from an audience, by very quick theatrical gestures used in a comedy way. Other sketches are much quieter. There are different shades, even within sketches. I played an old father in one sketch in *Behind the Fridge* and my character was a mixture of very farcical playing and clowning around, but I did try to make him a real character. Peter had the difficult task of being my son in that sketch and playing a rather earnest and sincere part.

P.C.: While around me was this chaotic, lunatic, seventy-year-old father whom I came to see because my mother had just died. I was a film star who couldn't be at the funeral or at his mother's side because he was on location in Yugoslavia. It was this terrible situation of apologizing for not being able to be there and so on.

D.M.: It was a family situation. But for me, the joy of the show was the fact of doing all sorts of characters. Not particularly diverse in accent or whatever, but the fact that in performing potential they were on different levels.

I love doing a show over and over again. Because you get to a point where a sketch gets to the essentials and really swings along. I would have loved to have seen some of the old music hall performers who'd been doing the same act for years and years and years, and knew exactly what was happening. And I really didn't get interested in the theatre till relatively late.

P.C.: I used to go and see the Crazy Gang as a sort of ritual, because my father worked in the Colonial Service and he was in Gibraltar at the time. I must have been about seven or eight, and whoever was putting me on the plane always used to take me to see the Crazy Gang, which was a different show every year.

D.M.: I saw Max Wall once on a radio show with Gert and Daisy.

P.C.: You saw him on a radio show, did you? That was clever.

D.M.: Yeah, I did.

P.C.: Oh, you went to a performance!

D.M.: The people I'm mentioning are people I like very much

but there are entertainers who do things I'm not mad about.

P.C.: Like Sammy Davis. The self-congratulation about his performance is appalling, I find. But then I'm a sour old bastard.

D.M.: But then Sammy Davis *is* tremendously sincere. I get overwhelmed by his massive sincerity.

P.C.: The massive sincerity with which he embraces Richard Nixon is something I find rather distressing. Formerly a Democrat. A great fighter for black people's rights, he then buys a house in the Bahamas, which is totally dominated by the whites.

D.M.: In the face of your consistency it must be rather appalling.

P.C.: I've been utterly consistent.

D.M.: Have you? How very boring.

P.C.: I've never embraced Richard Nixon or bought a house in the Bahamas.

D.M.: I wouldn't like to tell Ronald the things you have done.

R.H.: But is he consistent?

D.M.: A tricky question.

P.C.: I'll answer it for you. I'm not consistent.

D.M.: This is not my reply.

P.C.: I will argue for anything. Just for the sake of enjoying the argument I will take up any cause.

D.M.: Although you despise other people who do the same thing.

R.H.: How would you defend Sammy Davis Jnr?

P.C.: Well, I think he's absolutely right – a man who's devoted so much of his life to entertaining people should have his just reward in a house in the Bahamas, and I think it's an excellent place for him to be, and I think by mingling with the white people who dominate the power structure of the Bahamas he may be able to influence them and get a little more Black Power going. That's, I'm sure, Sammy's real reason for going over there.

R.H.: Would you agree with that?

D.M.: I think being in showbusiness – anyway Christ! I mean bloody hell – I'm very lucky, I think. We are, perhaps. I say 'perhaps' because I don't want to speak for Peter. But what an extraordinary profession to be in, really. Makes you feel quite queasy, the possibility that you *can* make a lot of money out of it.

P.C.: It's the same business as burglary really.

D.M.: I don't agree there.

P.C.: I think that's why showbusiness people and thieves get on so well.

R.H.: And what part do you think your influence has played in bringing Dudley Moore to his present self?

P.C.: Well, in depth analysis, which takes place almost daily, I play no part whatsoever.

D.M.: Peter, Peter!

P.C.: Except in getting very quarrelsome late at night.

D.M.: Which has brought me to my knees rather than to my inner self.

P.C.: Not at all.

D.M.: I didn't mean in supplication. I meant in fatigue.

P.C.: Of arguing endlessly. But cut arguing out of my life and I'd be lost.

D.M.: I don't think you would.

P.C.: You think I'd find myself.

D.M.: (*Harley Street voice*) I think this terrible fantasy of losing this pig-headedness, this inconsistent birkish argumentative quality – Sorry I've got to put it this way of course.

P.C.: It's only Freudian terms.

D.M.: Get stuffed, as Freud would say. No? Or rather yes.

ALEC GUINNESS

No living actor has succeeded better than Alec Guinness at creating characters without recognizable resemblance, facial or vocal to himself or to each other either. He has played both Richard II and Richard III; he has ranged from Hamlet to Sir Andrew Aguecheek. He reincarnated T. E. Lawrence in Terence Rattigan's *Ross* and Dylan Thomas in the one-man show *Dylan* in New York. His film characterizations range from Gully Jimson in *The Horse's Mouth* to Adolf Hitler, from Father Brown to the blustering Commanding Officer in *Tunes of Glory*. Jews and Arabs, crooks and diplomats, bigamists and cardinals – it is hard to think of any category of humanity Guinness has not penetrated with one of his characterizations.

But he no longer wants to use this almost endless capacity for disguising himself. 'I hope I do it less and less. At the time when I started in the theatre, in the early thirties, I was obviously not a straight, tennis-flannelled juvenile. That was simply going to be out. Neither had I got the kind of looks for any of that. Therefore you were what was called a character actor. What is more, in the sort of things I did in Gielgud's companies, you were required to play old men. This always happens in a big company: the old men are pretty well all played by the youngest members. I quavered around the place and I suppose I got into that habit really. And it amused me and I was very happy to disguise myself. I was always rather embarrassed with me personally, so to speak. I didn't quite know what all that was, and I was rather happy to go into a thin cardboard disguise. I think later one tried to make it a bit rounder, but it isn't something I've made a great fetish of. After the war, when I came out of the Navy, I did one show at Hammersmith and then went to the Old Vic and I didn't know whether my talent still existed, such as it was, or quite where it lay. I asked Olivier and Richardson, who were in charge of the company at that time, with John Burrell, "Look, please, on this first season may I have a very widely differing range of parts?" And indeed I did, and I thought that would solve the problem of where I was likely to go. But it didn't, because at the end I was happy in practically all those parts, having made a great effort to be different in each of them. The problem's drifted away now a bit, possibly through having greater confidence – though I can't think why I say that. There is no greater confidence – just greater laziness I suppose.'

Few of the actors and directors who have worked with him would accuse him of laziness, but a turning point did come for him when he hit on a saying of Chesterton's. 'It's revolution-ized my life – his remark that if a thing is worth doing, it's worth doing badly. I don't think I've ever been a perfectionist. I've been a worrier and a fusser, or niggly about things, but if only I'd come across that line of Chesterton's fifteen years ago it might have liberated me a great deal more, because there's a lot of stuff one can just chuck over one's shoulder and think "It's not going to be very marvellous this, anyway, but it's worth doing and so let it ride." It can of course also make for slightness, I suppose, and laziness, instead of that prissy "worth doing well" business, which is so puritanical. What's worth doing is worth doing.'

In talking to Guinness it soon becomes apparent that he is dissatisfied with most of his own achievements. 'I don't know that I look back on any of my performances with pleasure. I know ones I've enjoyed doing, obviously. But once it's done – that's it.' Although his Old Vic Richard II was extremely moving and quite unforgettable, he is highly disparaging about it. 'The echo of Gielgud's performance was too close to my ear and head without me re-thinking the part in my own terms or even in its own terms. It was a sort of pale *ersatz* – not even a shadow of Gielgud but attempting to be in that area. I thought so when I was doing it.' He is also critical of his performances as all nine victims of the murderer – includ-ing the female one – in the film *Kind Hearts and Coronets* (1949). 'I loved that film. I loved working with Robert Hamer, who became a dear friend and was a witty and interesting creature and, alas, no longer with us. But so far as the actual performing was concerned, it was pretty thin stuff, pretty cardboardy. I think the only sort of genuine one I did amongst that bunch was – I mean complete in itself – was the old vicar. But I'd already used all that before in something in the theatre. There was a little bit of a cheat somewhere along the line. Also, I rather fell between two stools, make-up-wise. Not that I did the make-up, but I thought some sort of family likeness should be retained amongst the characters when in fact I could have done a Lon Chaney job and made them all violently different. I don't know. I thought that Dennis Price was the person who gave a beautiful performance in that picture – it was so marvellously judged. I flipped on and off in a rather jokey way, let's face it.

'I thought *Tunes of Glory* was one of my better efforts and, although it was dismissed by the critics, I didn't think that Feisal in *Lawrence of Arabia* was all that bad. However, it was dismissed as funny accents, or something. On the other hand, I had a letter from some Arab princess saying "How did you manage to learn how my people walk?" That gave me enormous pleasure. One has one's private rewards now and then.'

Guinness began his career in an advertising agency. 'I started earning my living at eighteen or nineteen with a firm in Lincoln's Inn, first in copy-writing, then in layout and then back to copy-writing. They were all very kind to me but it hadn't been my ambition; it was a means of trying to earn a pound a week and eventually thirty shillings a week after eighteen months. The ambition was the theatre. Very consciously so, from the age of about fourteen, but I didn't realize that you did actually get properly paid. People, as they always do, said "Oh have a safe job. Go into a bank." Or something awful like that.

'Eighteen months in advertising was enough. I tried to get into RADA, but I had no money, so it meant trying for a scholarship, whatever I did, and I was all set. I was taken through my paces by Martita Hunt, whom I didn't know, for my RADA audition. But when I turned up at the appointed time, having paid the little fee, I was met by someone who said "Well, isn't it lucky you haven't come all the way down from Scotland? We've decided we're not giving any more scholarships this year." And I was left, flabbergasted, on the pavement. I'd got the afternoon off from the office, where there were obviously a lot of raised eyebrows and I was dreading having to go back there. Then I ran into a girl I used to know on the beach at Eastbourne when I was about fourteen or fifteen, and wept on her shoulder and she said "You'd better hurry, right now, round to the Fay Compton Studio in Baker Street because I know they're holding their auditions this afternoon". And I went bang straight there, went bang straight in, and got a scholarship. It was an extraordinary stroke of good fortune for me. Not that there was any money attached to the scholarship but at least I got a free training. Fay Compton herself rarely came to the Studio. She used to come and give away the prizes. Her sister, Vera, was a sort of Principal of the place. I think it was really very good.'

Guinness is aware of the relationship between acting and the games we play as children. 'We fool ourselves a great deal. I think a lot of acting, after all, is fooling oneself. It's even persuading yourself that you're a different character. You know jolly well you're not, but you have a great capacity, if you're a performer, for playing children's games, and how real do children think games are when they're playing them? It's the same thing, I think.'

Not that this is something he often thinks about. 'I'm working with professional grown-up actors and then it moves into a stage where you either are what could be called an artist or not. It's a matter of what you select and what you discard, and where you trim, and where you try and let something flow. It becomes a little bit different. Still, I think the springs lie either in the unhappiness and loneliness of childhood, making up stories for yourself and acting them out for yourself, or – for some people – in very happy childhoods of playing together. It can be one or the other.

'I suppose most actors suffer from a slight arrest of development. But I like actors as people. I find them just as real, in fact rather more real than people working in real estate or something. I find them alert on the whole. Not nearly so many of them are egomaniacs as is given out. I find they have far wider interests than would be expected. They're nearly always interested in the arts in some form, in painting or music.

They're very often greatly interested in sport. Some of them have wretchedly overexcited political views. I think they're inclined to be more alive than the stockbroker.'

It is also clear that the money factor does not bulk so large in their lives. 'It's easy to think that actors are there – if the going is good – to make some cash out of it, but it's impossible to think of an actor going into the theatre as a young man and thinking "Now I'm going to make some money". It's the last thing. There may be other despicable things tucked away which he's unaware of, but money can't be a motive.'

Guinness has a highly developed technique but little sympathy with actors who are merely 'technical'. 'I can think of one actor, who, when I'm watching him, makes me feel as if I'm being given an acting lesson. He's a brilliant actor, but I feel I'm being read a manual on every psychological aspect and I want to say "For God's sake, can't you just be it, act it, without dotting the i's and crossing the t's and ticking off the things in some text book?" I have much greater sympathy with barnstorming than that.'

Guinness's present inclination, as an actor, is towards simplifying, economizing, refining everything in the performance to a minimum. 'I'm greatly in love with a bare stage. I'm not in love with theatre-in-the-round, or projected things. I love a curtain to go up. I would have a brass band, if possible. In front of a red curtain with a gilded fringe along it, or a nice big whacking orchestra. I would even love to see people bothering to put on dinner jackets. That to me smells of the romance of the theatre, and there's not much of that left in the theatre. But once the curtain's gone up, I love something bare. I don't mean stark, but bare and simple. And I think that goes for the kind of acting I would like to do now – to cut out all unnecessary frills. I suppose there's a danger here of cutting away so much that there's nothing left that's apparent to other people. Nevertheless, it's an area that both interests and pleases me. To try and refine something down and eliminate the unnecessary. One can bewhisker oneself and benose oneself and do odd things with voice and legs and they can be very unnecessary. And you look at some beautiful, beautiful actor like Rex Harrison and you never catch him doing the unnecessary. Which is why it appears so effortless.

'When I did that rather odd *Macbeth* at the Royal Court in

1966 with Bill Gaskill directing, in a very, very interesting bare set, and a pretty young company, the great lesson was that the least frilly movement of a finger came out like a pistol shot. We rehearsed for a month or so, and we'd have really needed two or three months of rehearsal to eliminate – to be in that setting and to give the sort of performance that that production required. We were all too fussy. I don't think I was particularly so – I was a bit. But some of the less experienced ones didn't quite know how to eliminate. Gordon Jackson gave an absolutely beautiful performance. Came on and did nothing except intend and speak the lines, and I thought it was magical. And this is the sort of acting I'm in love with at the moment. I'm not saying I could do it. But that's my aim.'

There is a level, of course, at which it has always been his aim. 'I don't think there's been any turning point particularly. I did go to Japan in the early sixties for a holiday and saw some Noh theatre there. I was very impressed by the economy of the performance. Sometimes it's almost laughable. But also now and then it's hair-raisingly exciting, because of one small gesture, after nothing has happened for five minutes.

'It's awfully easy for actors to be naturalistic and do what is natural or what appears to be natural. And I think this can be awfully boring. I can see what's natural happening around me in restaurants and streets, and I think theatre should be something more of an art form. I think that Stanislavsky went too far.'

Guinness used to say that he could never play a character until he had mastered its walk, that he had to start from the feet up. But with his excellent characterization of Gully Jimson in *The Horse's Mouth* (1959), he had to start from the voice. 'I did the script of that myself, so I became very familiar with it, but I had one technical problem to face up to – the voice. I thought "Once that's solved I hope the rest of it will fall into place". It wasn't a question of the grittiness of the voice so much as the accent. Because it seemed to me that it had to be educated, and yet if you spoke with an educated accent, a lot of the lines and a lot of the situations became not quite believable. If you Cockneyed it up a bit, it was false to the book, and so I tried to find a voice in which no one would be able to detect an accent of any sort. Gritty, rough . . . more or less air passing over gravel. Eventually I did find a voice which made me think "I'll have to use that". Then I felt myself free just to relax and say the lines and *be* it. I also thought of appearance. I wanted a wig to make me look rather like Stanley Spencer. Not that the character is anything to do with Stanley Spencer, but a photograph of Stanley Spencer made me think that this would solve the hair problem, and then it was just a matter of buying rather nasty, cheap boots and boiling them. Actually stirring them round in the kitchen in vast saucepans. I didn't really think about the movement at all.'

In John Mortimer's play *A Voyage Round My Father* (1971) the main technical problem for Guinness lay in the blindness of the central character. 'Well, you can make a clinical study of a blind man. I suppose I'm capable of doing that, tapping my way around. I know one or two blind people and I know exactly what goes on with their eyes, which are kind of dead, and the kind of turned-up thing that happens. One could spend an evening being so clinically blind that one wouldn't get on with the acting of it – also it's a bit off-putting. So I played with my eyes fractionally open and doing what I think suggests blindness with them. I spent a good deal of time in rehearsal doing it with my eyes shut – to get the feel. And I was amazed at how quickly I found my way around the stage – mind you with not much furniture – and found where people were without actually falling into them. Someone said to me "Are you going to do so much of it with your eyes shut? Because it creates a slightly sleepy feeling". It had gone through my mind. I wonder if you see someone with their eyes shut – even if they're talking vigorously – whether you begin to doze. So then I was faced with having to select, and actually place where I could have my eyes open a bit more. I thought "Need I go through this whole process of him being blind totally? Can I just have them open or just half open?"

'The voice and eyes, apart from one's actual physical presence, are the two main things. And to act this part one had to kiss one of them goodbye. I would ordinarily try and get a laugh purely on a look, and I couldn't do that. And the voice in this particular case had to have a certain harshness, a bludgeoning quality about it, which gave me less freedom than I would ordinarily have in using it.'

Though the play was largely autobiographical, Guinness did not attempt a portrait of Mortimer's father. 'I've looked at lots of photographs of his father, but I didn't make any effort to look like him, except that I wore the same sort of clothes and a slight modification of the hair-do he had. Not that that counts much in this case. Neither Leueen McGrath, who played the mother, nor I were doing anything about that. I did find out from John Mortimer some little characteristics his father had. When he was cross-examining, he always stood with his hands folded on his tummy. I don't know why, but that's rather good. I might have had my hands behind my gown or anything. But it suddenly did something – created a certain little relaxed thing from which the insistence of cross-examination cut across rather surprisingly. One or two small things like that do give a feeling of solidity. But they could have been observed from anyone, really.'

For any actor who loves the theatre as much as Guinness but has as much success in the cinema, the problem of apportioning time between the two can be agonizing. 'I think I'm lucky to get what work I do, really. There are so many actors out of work. Of course I'm interested in earning an income. But I think if someone said to me "Now listen, you've got to do one or the other", I would settle for the theatre. I regret having given so much time to the cinema. I've made some pretty lousy films, partly because of having contracts to fulfil. You think "Well, I don't know, it's not terribly good but the next one might be even worse, so I'd better do this." It's a great mistake, seeking security by saying "Yes, I'll have a big contract for four pictures. That will do splendidly." And then grumbling at what you find yourself doing. I've had some really lucky contracts, which I've been very happy doing, but I do wish I'd been a bit more courageous in saying "Well, I don't know, just let it ride", and given a bit more time to the theatre in the last fifteen years. Mind you, I do more theatre than people realize. Every year I do something in the theatre. And basically I like being my own master.

'In films, you're at the mercy of what happens in the cutting-room. You haven't got control of the set-up. Of course you haven't total control of the set-up in the theatre. But you have a co-operative working out of things. If you've got a good director it works out well. With cinema directors you notice their names are getting bigger and bigger on the bills, and quite rightly so. It's their medium. The actor is either a type or a suitable someone-or-other who has no final control even over his own performance. In the theatre he has. I mean a director might say "I think that's lousy" or "I suggest we cut this". Well, you tailor your resulting performance accordingly. In the cinema, I've been so caught out at times by something disappearing in a performance which I was relying on, that I would have played the whole thing differently had I known that particular thing was going to go. That happens so often. Of course the disappearance of some things can improve the film and so the performance. But the performance would have been even better could the wretched actor have known what he was doing.'

In filming even the duration of a pause can be determined in the cutting-room. 'The whole thing of acting really is timing, particularly in comedy, obviously. And even that you can be robbed of. In one film I was in, which I disliked thoroughly, I knew that there was a reasonable laugh in a certain area if just left quietly to itself. And indeed, when it came to seeing rushes at an early stage, there was. But the money-bags boys interfered. "No, we want a big gag there." So they put in someone else's legs going yuuummmp down a ladder and then bonk at the end of it – because that was their idea of a laugh. And in the cinema it got a dead cold withdrawal from the audience, because they couldn't believe – I would like to think – that I would do that. And they were quite right. I didn't even know it was in the film. And a very well known film magnate said to me once "Give us some pratfalls, Alec, get us some laughs." Well I love pratfalls, but I'm not very good at doing them, so I'm not the person to ask.

'I'm not jaded about doing anything like that, but when he gets to pushing the late fifties, I think any actor – certainly myself – gets a bit alarmed as to how their memory is going to serve them in the future. I've had no trouble so far. But with every job I think now this may be the one in which I can't retain the lines sufficiently. You can *know* them, but they simply don't come out. So you can't rely on that. Of course, once that happens, small bits in films are the answer.'

Guinness does not miss the eye-contact with a live audience.
'People seem to think that when you're filming you've got no
audience. But of course you have, a very experienced audience
of about a hundred people watching you all the time. They
don't laugh but I don't think that matters. You jolly well
know the feeling of either suppressed amusement, or interest,
or sheer boredom. They can't disguise it. Their faces may
remain blank, but you get it.'

In the theatre, too, an actor in Guinness's position can say
'yes' to a leading part in a play by an important writer, only to
wish he had said 'no'. Guinness, retrospectively, does not set a
high valuation on Arthur Miller's *Incident at Vichy*. 'I thought
it had a noble intention. That was about it. But I got some
very curious postcards from people saying "Who cares about
Jews being burnt up in furnaces?" "Why do you play in this
rubbish?" These made me feel the play was worth doing. No
one in their senses would write like that, whatever their
racialist or political feelings, but it's the sort of mental sick-
ness that there is walking around.'

Generally the actor can do a great deal towards controlling
the sympathy that the audience is going to feel towards a
character. There are some actors who maintain that it is
necessary to love each character they play and look at everything from his point of view, however much they dislike it.
Guinness does not agree with this. 'I think you're bound to
make some sort of a comment on the character. I would have
thought total identification was crazy. There must be an
element of comment, either sympathetic or alienated. But you
must be able to alienate, you can't sympathize with all parts.
And the audience is not meant to sympathize with all parts,
for heaven's sake. They're meant to be nauseated or horrified
by out-and-out villains. I've no idea how this is achieved.
Whether it's through total identification or alienation. You
couldn't play certain comic or amusing characters in Sheridan
without seeing them through a kind of diminishing glass,
through a kind of lorgnette, something that puts them rather
at a remove, so that they become insect-like. You can't go into
their full lives and sympathize. You're not meant to, there
isn't time, it's not the style of the job and these things vary
from entertainment to entertainment.'

PETER NICHOLS

Like David Mercer and Charles Wood, Peter Nichols established himself as a television playwright before emerging as one of the pace-setters in the British theatre. *A Day in the Death of Joe Egg* was produced in the West End in July 1967, eleven days before his fortieth birthday. But whereas Mercer has so far made more formal experiments on television than in the theatre, Peter Nichols's television plays have been comparatively straightforward: altogether he finds himself unable to feel as much commitment to the medium as he does to the theatre. 'You can't give the same attention to it as you do to the stage. I regard films in the same way, I suppose. People pay attention to the writer when he's writing for the stage, and to a lesser extent when he's writing for television, and to no extent at all in films. The director has taken over entirely. And with television, the difference is simply the old thing of the play not being repeated, not being there, as an object, when you want to see it. *The Heart of the Country* is a good example. It described about a year of my life, and you throw that away on one television play. It's not like a novel. If nobody buys a novel, at least it's there on a shelf and someone could notice it eventually. They even wipe the tapes of TV plays.'

The first play he wrote for the stage was called *The Continuity Man* (1963). 'It was commissioned by a West End manager and as I had an Arts Council bursary, I was able to take some time off from telly and write it. But nobody wanted to do it. Then, ironically enough, a TV producer got hold of it and asked me if I'd do it for television. So I knocked it down in length and it was done for television. It was very good as such. That was the first play I did with Christopher Morahan, who has since directed, I think, five of my TV plays.'

The Heart of the Country was typical of his work in incorporating autobiographical material. 'I haven't managed to break away from that. I'm always rather half-heartedly complaining about it, but I don't know that the complaints are entirely sincere – because you just write what you can write, don't you? I do feel that *The National Health* (1969) was a breakaway from that, but now I've started again with *Forget-Me-Not-Lane* (1971). One of the reviews of *A Day in the Death of Joe Egg* in America complained that I had so far seemed to be a writer who just dealt in autobiography. And when you first read something like that you think "Oh yes, that's true". I'd like to change in the sense that it's very *obviously* autobiography. Everybody writes autobiography, but a lot of writers manage to clothe it in disguises of various kinds. With me there's no disguise. My parents, friends and brothers can recognize themselves in what I write. It's rather obvious and rather painful too.'

Though *The National Health* derives from prolonged experience of various hospitals, it is less directly autobiographical than *Joe Egg*, which could have been written only by the parent of a spastic child. 'It called for very direct description of the subject, and its directness is what made it work on the stage – standing there and saying "And then we did this and then we did that". Even though the characters themselves weren't really like us. I wrote a first draft in which the characters were more like me and my wife, and then I thought "This is not working, because it's notoriously fatal to try to write yourself into a play". You either tend to come out like a hero or a knocked down, neutral character. Because you can't really see yourself. I thought, "What if this experience had happened to another person? I can't hear myself and I want a tone of voice that I can hang on to". And I did this – I imposed another person's manner of speaking on the play. I just happened to have this friend who seemed to me to be rather amusing, to have an interesting turn of phrase. Actually, the hero, Bri, turned out not to be like him either, but that's what I thought it would be, and it got me away from writing in my own tone of voice.

'I'm really a mimic. I can only do it as long as I'm mimicking somebody. I couldn't write novels because I have to imitate other people. Then again the characters in my plays are always imitating each other. I mean I'm imitating as I'm writing and then they themselves, in character, imitate other people. In *Joe Egg*, a man takes on the identity of a parson, a doctor and so on. I was an actor for five years, though I never wanted to be, particularly. I always wanted to be a writer. I used to do concert parties with my mother during the war, entertaining the troops. I used to do a Stanley Holloway monologue. Then I joined the Air Force and went over to Singapore and got into Combined Services Entertainment, which came after ENSA. I worked with Kenneth Williams and Stanley Baxter and John Schlesinger in and out of drag up and down Malaya and across to Hong Kong. And then I came home and went to the Bristol Old Vic School for two years and afterwards tried to be an actor for about five years. I gave it up because I was unsuccessful and couldn't earn a living, so I went to a training college and became a teacher. And while I was teaching I wrote my first television play in the evenings. I'd been writing plays all the time, but this was the first I submitted, and the BBC accepted it, so I wrote another which was taken by Granada and I gave up teaching, after about two years of it, and went to live in the country. That's how *Heart of the Country* was written. I got married at the same time. But we gradually drifted back from the country to Bristol again, where I'd started from. Finally, we came to live in Blackheath.'

It is sometimes said that the reason our post-war theatre has developed in the way it has is that so many of our playwrights, having themselves been actors, have written from the actor's point of view – Pinter, Osborne, Whiting, Orton, and many others. But as Peter Nichols sees it, the empathizing required of the playwright has more to do with mimicry than with acting. 'It's the difficulty of putting yourself into the other person.' But his talent as a mimic was of little help to him when he was trying to earn a living as an actor. 'People weren't writing the kind of things that I could imitate. It was mimicry for me to go on and be a juvenile lead, I suppose, in a sense. I was doing an imitation of people I had seen playing juvenile leads. I was happier in character parts, grotesques.'

Peter Nichols's habit of making his characters talk directly to the audience is much more than a stylistic device. It conditions his whole technique as a playwright, and it helps him to achieve a much closer relationship with his audience. It is no accident that he emerged into prominence at the time when fashion was swinging away from picture-frame theatres and the rigid separation that the proscenium imposes between the actor and the audience.

A Day in the Death of Joe Egg begins rivetingly with an effect which Nichols could never have achieved on television. Bri talks to the audience as if it were a class in a schoolroom. Nichols would never have written in this manner if he had not been a performer. 'It was a sketch I'd written and performed at parties when I'd been a teacher. Then I took the jokes out of it because it wasn't meant to be a comic turn. I'd wanted the man just to be desperate at the end of the week and the end of the term – Christmas, harassed teaching, trying to cope with it. But I wanted to make the audience laugh at it. And then he goes home, and what's he got to face him when he gets home? A hopelessly crippled daughter.'

The director of a playwright's first play and the casting of the leading part can have a big effect not only on the niche the play finds for itself, but on the writer's subsequent development. Joe Melia, who played Bri in Michael Blakemore's original production at the Glasgow Citizens' Theatre, was a performer with more experience of revue than of drama. 'Casting Joe in it helped us a lot more, then Michael deciding to use music made it more acceptable that he should speak to the audience. These were all little bricks to build up the whole effect.'

In the New York production Albert Finney played Bri. 'He was very different. Very good. I'm never sure really, whether one was better than the other. Joe's got a remarkable quality about him. With Albert our difficulty, of course, was to imagine him being unsuccessful with women. Everybody said this. When he sat down and said "Three out of God knows how many tens of thousands I've tried", you thought "Well, I can't quite believe that". Because he was so obviously sexually attractive, confident, a golden boy. But he played it very well and succeeded, oddly enough, in parts that I didn't think Joe was particularly good in, though we thought he would be. Joe's revue turns were very good but Albert did more to make them real. He actually did more studied impersonations.

Whereas Joe did it all from his own personality. What Joe's got is a kind of other sense. All the time he's acting, you feel he's also with you saying "Look at this". He's got a sort of objectivity about his acting – he doesn't identify with his character. He's a comic in that way. He stands back. And yet, strangely enough, this worked very well in the latter part of the play, which was more serious, when the situation had really got a hold, when he did all the running about and the attempted murder very well, I thought. It was very moving. It was difficult to know how the whole thing would work. I remember Joe up in Glasgow saying "I think they'll be laughing for the first ten minutes, and then, when we bring the child on, it will STOP like that and there'll be no more laughter". And sure enough, when they brought the child on, they did stop laughing and then we thought "Well, are they going to laugh again or are we going to go through the whole play without another titter?" And they started again. They had to accept both at the same time.'

One important side of Peter Nichols's development as a playwright has been his gradual refinement of the revue technique he introduced into *Joe Egg*. In *The National Health* it is Barnet, the hospital porter, who enters into the same sort of relationship with the audience that a comedian has. His function is partly choric, and he also helps to bridge the gap between the reality of the hospital and the fantasy parallel which takes the characters into the world of *Emergency Ward 10* and *Dr Finlay's Casebook*, television glamorizations of medical routines. Once again the director, Michael Blakemore, and his casting of another comedian (Jim Dale) in the key role, had a strong influence on the final result we saw on the stage. 'I didn't originally have Barnet, the porter, reading the comic TV bits. They were written for a Narrator, but Michael said "Look, I think we can use Barnet to do this, particularly if we get a comedian to play the part". And we were lucky enough to have Jim Dale, and he could do this wonderful swift transition and speak in a quasi-American dialect. He was able to move in and out of the action and come down and get a microphone, and comment on it. And it worked very well.'

Much always depends on the physical limitations and amenities of the theatre. At the Old Vic there is a large trapdoor which made it possible for all the fantasy sequences to be brought up on a lift from below. 'I hadn't written it like that. My original intention was that it just came trundling on. They brought on one or two things that they needed. Everything else in the play moves on wheels – the beds, the trolleys, the apparatus, the screens. Everything is brought on and off, so that at the end the stage is empty. That was going to happen with the TV scenes. But Michael said "Why do that when we've got these lovely trapdoors that come up with the props on?" So that divided it more clearly. It meant that when something came up from underneath, you realized it was bound to be part of the fantasy – not a real hospital. An awful lot of the specific arrangements – where people went down the front steps, where they went off to the side, were changed in the course of rehearsals. It was a very elaborate production. We did a lot of drill, a terrific lot of hard work. It was like Sandhurst – which is one of Michael's strong points. He just runs through these things one after the other. It means that whatever else happens, you can be quite sure the mechanics are going to work. Nothing is left to chance in his productions.'

One of the advantages for a playwright in having his work done as part of a repertoire is that the actors do not become stale from having to go through the same lines and movements eight times a week. One of the disadvantages is that the play receives only two or three performances each week. 'And so you lose the impetus of the original notices. It comes out, you get your notices, you get the publicity. And quickly other plays come on and get their publicity and people forget about your play. They took off *National Health* for three months because the company had to go to America. When it came back they had to pick up and start from scratch again. And then off in the summer – and on again in the autumn, and we kept thinking "It's never going to pull itself up off the ground". And when it was in that season at the Cambridge Theatre, the show never recovered its impetus. But when it came back to the Vic, it did well again. This is the disadvantage. The advantage is that the company can think in between, and start again, refreshed. They're not tempted to start trying to get extra laughs in the wrong place. They improved it enormously: the precision in the performance towards the end of the run was wonderful. They knew exactly where to wait, where to place the laughs. So that the people who came a year after the opening were actually getting the best of the bargain. I don't think it will ever be done as well as that again.'

They were lucky to have so many actors in the company who were ideal for the main parts. 'We had a Welshman in the play and there was Gerry James in the company, a marvellous actor. We had a Scots surgeon and there was Paul Curran. You know, the casting just went on like that. We had Jim Dale and Robert Lang. It wasn't quite as easy as I'm making out, because they were trying to divide the companies, so they could take one on tour and keep other plays going. One of the reasons my play kept being taken off was that it had actors from each company. Some were in the Maggie Smith half and some in the other half. So when they went off to do Maggie Smith's plays in America, half the actors went with them and we had to drop the play. You think "God, I've got a choice of eighty actors at the National Theatre here". Then you realize that if you want to keep your play running all the time, you've only got a choice of forty and they may not be the best casting. So Michael and I had an awful lot of pushing and shoving. Pushing Olivier, pushing other people in order to get the actors we wanted.'

The play was commissioned by the National Theatre. 'But I didn't really consciously write it for those actors. Because it was already a television play called *The End Beds*, which I'd written years ago, and which had been rejected, because they thought it was going to be depressing. That didn't include the porter or the television scenes, but the realistic part was similar and the characters were more or less the same. I didn't think "Oh, they've got Gerald James, so I'll write a Welshman". I wrote a Welshman and was happy enough to have Gerald James there.'

One sequence which rather misfired in the production at the National was the one in which the porter wrecks the cured alcoholic's chances of staying off the bottle. 'This was partly because of Jim Dale's performance – he can't help being attractive. I think Jim's aware that he makes this impression, and he seized rather too much, I thought, on that moment at the end. In fact I wrote a lot of it out: there was less in it at the end than there was at the beginning. The nastiness, when it actually came on, was too strong and it twisted the whole play. I don't really see Barnet, the porter, as nasty. I just see him as a survivor. Not that he expresses my point of view at all. People often took lines out of his mouth and said "This is presumably what the author means. There's something bent about the healing arts". I don't think that, but this is what he thought. I wanted him to be somebody who survived at all costs. He's a bloke who's in control. If the play represents anything about England or the world you can meet in hospital, he was the sort of strong, continuing element of ordinary, vulgar, vigorous life that finds its way through all these institutions and survives. Makes a bit of money out of gambling, you know, a bit of this, a bit of the other. Hasn't got any liberal views about curing alcoholics or anything. He just thinks "Bloody hell, he's an alcoholic. If he wants some money for a drink I'll give it to him". But Jim did a slightly evil-genius thing, which I didn't really go along with.

'But altogether I lose sympathy towards the end of the play. Michael and I both felt that somehow or other we'd slightly missed the target. My impression was that it began very well, took a dip somewhere, picked up again, continued quite strongly and then went down towards the end and never recovered. That's always been my feeling.'

The play handles a much bigger group of characters than *Joe Egg* and inevitably concerns itself with them less intimately. 'Rather like going along in a train and glimpsing a lot of things. You see somebody working in a garden. A woman washing her windows. You see kids playing. You get a glimpse of each of these and you think "Let's see what kind of life she must lead. Ah yes, I can see he's just got home". But you're not really deeply involved with any of them. What you do is glimpse their past life through the little peep they give you. Which is the way it seems in hospital or an institution where you meet people casually. And suddenly, for no reason, there is a great eruption of passion about nothing at all. Apparently. A basket or a bedpan. They don't actually say "My God, what I wanted to do in life was so-and-so and look what's happened to me". This is a different sort of playwriting. Not an Arthur Miller sort of playwriting, where the events are put forward and woven into a tight structure. In this play, suddenly, a little flash of something happens, and then it just disintegrates into concern about how to get from here to there again, or how to get your pyjamas on, or whether you've got to go down to physiotherapy. And those things take over again. A comic way of writing, I suppose. A number of things are repeated, then finally you can get so many of them going that they can finally all be thrust on one at the same time and it becomes almost funny, because you're not having time to sympathize with each one. It's all too swift. Like the scene when a man's dying of cancer. It's a terrible shame, but you're not deeply enough involved with him. What you do bring to it are your own feelings, as an audience, about cancer. You don't really think deeply about that man, because you don't know much about him. But then another man is on a bedpan so you laugh at that. And then a doctor is falling asleep because he hasn't had enough time off duty and you laugh at that. And then, oh, cancer again! So that you're being continually kept in a state of comic alarm. You don't have time to think "I'm not really finding out a lot about these people". It's only afterwards you think "What *do* we know about them?" And then you try to piece it all together.'

One of the difficulties of writing a train-window-viewpoint play is that the question remains of who is looking out of the train window. 'I think this is always a problem in writing – who's seeing it, whose viewpoint is it? And the other one is the time element. Graham Greene said it was a great problem for novelists, but I think it's a problem for all fiction writers. How do you condense? How do you cheat about time and make it all happen in two hours? How does time pass? *Forget-Me-Not-Lane* is much more directly concerned with that, because it's a memory play.

'It covers twenty years in two hours, and the actors are continually coming in in the present, then going out and coming back in the past. This is actually playing with what is really a serious problem for the writer, thumbing your nose at the problem. Saying "If I can't beat you, I'll make fun of you". I think the viewpoint for *National Health* was simply the audience. We're sitting in the theatre. We're not a fly on the wall of the hospital. If we were, that man would never come forward and speak to us. We wouldn't have all those irrelevant elements.

'It's amazing what you can do once you decide that the naturalistic convention is a convention, a device. People complain that they're fed up with this "device" of people talking to the audience. In fact if they had *not* talked to the audience that would have been a device. Because they would have had to pretend that the audience wasn't there. Of course they would have listened for their laughs and waited until they'd stopped laughing and then gone on. So it's artificial. But still a partial pretence. But if you say "Part of the time we'll have that pretence, and part of the time we'll drop the pretence and talk to the audience" it's amazing the things that can result from this. In *Joe Egg* they used to come forward sometimes and talk to the audience, indeed two of them talked to the audience through most of the first act. In *Forget-Me-Not-Lane* people do it the whole way through, and when they can't cope with the people on the stage they turn to the audience. You can have a long scene in which there may be people arguing with each other. Perfectly content to – and then they'll come forward and appeal to the audience, as though they're uninvited guests who have just been sitting there, watching the terrible row.'

It might seem from this as though Peter Nichols, who had written about fourteen television plays before *Joe Egg* was staged in 1967, had been terribly frustrated by the impossibility of making direct contact with the audience. 'But I didn't feel that, quite honestly. My first plays were written in a rather cool way. I started off modelling them on Italian films. I wrote a play called *Promenade*, which was much influenced by Fellini's *I Vitelloni*, about a group of layabouts in Brighton. But after that I just wrote in a sort of *Coronation Street* or *Z Cars* style. Even in 1970 I went back and did this entirely straight play about a funeral, *Hearts and Flowers*, which was absolute keyhole stuff really – a small chain of human behaviour and no talking to the camera or anything like that. I don't think it works terribly well on television. There's something wrong with this attitude, I know, because most of the time on television people are talking directly to us – David Frost, and the newsreader, and the weatherman. Even though we're not there. They're obviously *not* talking to us because they don't know who the hell we are, but they're talking to a camera. It's perhaps the camera that worries me. The fact that I know they're not talking to me. But actors can turn and talk to the audience and, if the lights suddenly went on they could see us all, and if we laugh, they've got to respond. The responses of Jim Dale to the women in the audience weren't something he made up. They were written into the play. "There's a lady down there knows what I mean".'

Hearts and Flowers was an offshoot of *Forget-Me-Not-Lane*. 'I started to write *Forget-Me-Not-Lane*, got bogged down and couldn't see my way. So I turned aside and wrote a television play about the funeral of the father I was trying to write about in the stage play. The man is already dead when the television play starts. And *Forget-Me-Not-Lane* is about the life of the father – and other people of course. The funeral is also just briefly mentioned, so that one could say "See the television play for details." I treat a television play as an essay. I don't regard it as finished, because I can use the material again. Refine it. Mix it up. Intensify it, and I hope improve it. *Forget-Me-Not-Lane* is actually a kind of mixture of *Continuity Man* and a play called *When the Wind Blows*.'

Peter Nichols describes his plays as 'efforts to find out how worthwhile an idea is. Is it something that preoccupies me a good deal?' A question that has preoccupied him for years is how deeply we are conditioned by childhood experience. 'How much can we escape from the early years? I don't think we can really. And to what extent should we be glad? To what extent should we try and think of another way of living? And the way we go on caring.'

Just as Arthur Miller found that having children of his own changed his attitude to his father, Nichols found his was changed by the fact of becoming a father himself. 'You start to see one more generation forwards. We are different, and yet we're remarkably similar. I find myself all the time feeling like my father. The older I get, the more I feel like him. The more I can understand him now. That I've got a body that's ageing, that I'm not a young man any more. I look at my children and I see them observing us. In *Forget-Me-Not-Lane* the husband says "And I saw my thirteen-year-old boy watching my wife and me growling and roaring at each other". And I thought "What can we make of this?" Just as a minute ago we saw him watching his parents quarrelling, because I'd got all the play's events mixed up on stage so you're never quite sure where you are. And because of that you can put the two things very close together and see them. It's as though you took two sections of your life, one very early and one very late on, put them together and showed their relationship. But it's all comic too – this has to be said. I don't know how deeply I could go into it if I tried to write a serious play. But I don't write particularly serious plays. They're written in a comic tone, aren't they? We don't have much discussion at rehearsals about what the play means or what the characters are about. We try to get the comedy right. And if that works we think the play will work. Whereas in an Arthur Miller play you might stop and all have to sit down and say "Now let's see about this relationship".'

Obviously, serious points can be made in comic terms, but even in *Joe Egg* Nichols feels that he was limiting the depth of the play by making himself take a comic view. 'You could take a serious view in which I think you could get deeper into the situation. I think you could say "Well look, I feel terrible about this". And nobody ever says that in the play. They keep it strictly on a level of what you could say to your friends or what you could say to other people. Social.' When he compares God to a manic-depressive rugby football player who uses us for a ball, Nichols may be making essentially the same point Shakespeare was making in *King Lear* when he said 'As flies to wanton boys are we to the gods', but certainly the two lines carry very different emotional loads. In *Joe Egg*, as Nichols says, 'You don't feel "Oh God!" You laugh at it, and then you go "Ugh! A bit too true to be funny". Afterwards.'

The National Health is even more detached than *Joe Egg*, but this is partly because it was based on emotional food which had been cooked and got cold a very long time ago. 'I had, really, very little feeling about *The National Health*. When I rewrote the original television play, it was really a question of "How can I make this work? What does it mean? Why am I writing about a hospital?" And I didn't answer this to my own satisfaction at all. But I had this idea that it gives, somehow or other, an impression of life in England, seen in this very specific way. And I was conscious of this and I think it guided the way I wrote the episodes. But I tried never to lose sight of the fact that these were the real people I had seen in hospital. Although I hadn't particularly liked them as

men, when I met them, and I hadn't got involved with them at
all. They were, literally, men I met and moved away from.
In a number of hospitals, at different times. At the same time,
in the course of writing, I got to know them. And rather
liked them. Simply because of being amused by them. This
helped an awful lot. I don't know that I'd like to spend very
much time with any of them, but it's a funny process. You
get to understand them. But it wasn't anything that I felt
terribly strongly about. In *Joe Egg* I had to control my feelings. I had to say "Don't say that, even if you feel it. Because
it's not going to work. Aesthetically it's going to stick out.
This tone must be maintained." And I think it worked because
the tone *was* maintained. Had we dropped the mask, it
wouldn't have worked. It only worked because we could keep
it up.'

Though *The National Health* is less directly autobiographical
than *Joe Egg*, the characters in it are much closer to their real-
life counterparts, because Peter Nichols works – as he always
has – from a diary. 'And I go back and look at the little bit I
wrote about people and from this I construct a character. This
is why on the whole I write about the family, because the
family obviously occurs most in the diary. I give them different names each time and hope they'll look different when
they're played by different actors, but they're always a bit the
same. But I didn't have much down about these men. For
instance, the alcoholic – there really was such a man, and he
really said quite a few of the things he said in the play. But I
was in India for three years in the Air Force, and listened to
the men talking and put in a lot of that stuff. That I know that
man could have said. So gradually he was fabricated on the
basis of the character I met in hospital. All my plays are
written from the diary. Sometimes it's only one page I use
for a whole play. Sometimes it's ten pages. In the case of the
funeral, for instance, it's almost exactly as it was in the diary,
and there are certain points I head for. But then there might
be another funeral – of somebody else – on another page, from
which I will take one detail. And then there'll be a party – it
was in fact a wedding party – where I can use something for
the funeral party. It's like a mosaic or collage. I write bits
down and then stick a bit on that . . . it's a very technical,
cold process.' The results, however, are not at all cold.

If the process of working from the diary is partly editorial, the play then goes through a second stage of being edited in collaboration with Michael Blakemore, who is one of the few practising directors to have enjoyed any success as a writer. He has published a long novel about actors. 'We work quite a lot on the script before we get to the draft that we want to rehearse. He's very good at that. With *Forget-Me-Not-Lane* I did several drafts before I showed it to him. And then he read it and suggested some improvements. We discussed that. And then a few more. Then we decided it was all right and we put it to the management. They said yes, they'd like to do it. This play was written for the Greenwich Theatre initially. And then Michael came back and said "I've had some more thoughts – I think this could go and that could go". But we like to get to the script we're actually going to rehearse by the time we're casting, so that we don't give the actors one script to read and then say "Sorry, that's been cut". This is awful, because then they don't know whether to accept the part or not. Often you feel like changing it again, but it's best not to, I think.'

They do still make small changes once the play has gone into rehearsal. 'But they are very small. For instance in moving *Joe Egg* from Glasgow to London we changed the last two pages. That's all. So as just to have the child on the stage at the end. Originally the mother came home leaving the child in hospital. They had their last scene in which she unwittingly suggests to Bri that there's no solution. And he decides that he's going to go anyway. We see that he's leaving her because he picks up his suitcase and says he's just going to make a telephone call. He goes off. She comes on and says "Ah, what a Daddy! Aren't we lucky?" to herself, and to the fish, and the cat. She goes upstairs. But we later thought we must have the child on, because she's the dominating figure in the play even though she doesn't do anything. We need to see her last of all. So we decided after Glasgow that we would have Sheila bringing the child back from the hospital. It's perfectly feasible. They wheel her into the centre and have to talk around her, just as at the beginning. Saying "Hullo, lovely. How are you? You're all right. You look well". And then he goes off, with the suitcase. She comes back and says to the child "What a Daddy, aren't we lucky?" And *then* goes off.

This was one of those cases where it just clicked. It was better.'

Peter Nichols mostly writes every day. 'I sit for hours without writing anything. And I must say that things occur to me in scenes. I think "That would be a good scene" long before I think "I will write a play about a spastic child". There's a television play, *The Gorge* (1965), which started out with a picnic. "I must write a picnic scene in one of my plays." And then when they asked me to do a television play, I thought "I'll do the whole thing as a picnic". And then I had to go around and find out what else was going to happen. And eventually the picnic turns out to be just one of the scenes. The story is of a family who go to picnic in the Mendips. Several other families also picnic, and events arise out of that. Nobody would be able to guess what it had started with. I think writers do this quite a lot.'

His method of working has hardly changed at all since he turned to writing professionally at the end of the fifties. 'I think Anthony Trollope said at the end of his life that something that took six months at the beginning he could then have written in six weeks. Simply because he'd learnt how to do things. I've certainly done that. But I don't know in what way. I couldn't tell anyone anything at all about playwriting. I've just got no view of it. I only know when it's working. I think this is a drawback. I'd like to be able to say "I feel strongly about this, and I'd like to write a play about it". And be able then to say "Yes, these are the elements that I want to include" – and proceed on a very logical constructional basis. But I don't do that. I think "I must head for that scene. What am I going to do in between?" Often the things that fill in turn out to be just as good as the scenes I was heading for. But it is an endless process of artificial respiration, slapping dead flesh into life. It may be a drawback I'm stuck with for life. But I intend next time, if I can, to work more logically, with more idea of what I'm trying to head for.

'I must say there's a great deal of pleasure, of sheer literary enjoyment, in the actual writing. Imitating voices, using words that I wouldn't know how to use unless the character had used them. In *Forget-Me-Not-Lane* the father's making a list of things he doesn't like. He lists a lot of ludicrous things and then he breaks off and says "Where was I?" And Ursula says "Dirty fingernails" and he says "Bartok". Just about the last

word you'd expect. That's just the pleasure of tricking the
audience. My father really made these ludicrous lists. He was
a commercial traveller and such a funny man that one could
more or less put anything into his mouth and it works. In a
different milieu he'd have been a grand eccentric like Sitwell's
father. Once, when I was sharing a London flat with another
fellow, my old man came to visit. And my friend said afterwards that he felt as though he'd met Micawber. . . .

'I was shocked when the notices for the play said I'd
obviously loathed my father, because in the last years of his
life I grew very fond of him. He's been in three of my plays
now, and in *Hearts and Flowers* he was a corpse. So perhaps
he won't crop up again. You can't be sure. This is what I
meant by bringing him back again and again in *Forget-Me-
Not-Lane* until his son finally shouts: "You're dead, so go!" '

GÜNTER GRASS

Poet, playwright, novelist, painter, sculptor, pamphleteer, ex-jazz musician, Günter Grass is not only one of the most exuberantly versatile figures on the contemporary scene, he is also one of the most deeply committed. As George Steiner put it, 'Much of what is the active conscience in the Germany of Krupp and the Munich beer halls lies in this man's ribald keeping'. In *The Tin Drum*, a novel which has been translated into fifteen languages and sold over one and a half million copies, Grass's dwarfish drummer, Oskar Matzerath, refuses to grow up into the intolerable world of the Third Reich. Grass has said that he was influenced by *Tristram Shandy* but whereas Sterne plays chronological tricks by making himself very visible as narrator, precariously preserving his balance while dexterously tangling both feet in an increasingly complicated storyline, Grass dons one of the most improbable disguises in Western fiction, transforming himself into a dwarf who can shatter glass with his scream and beat on a magic drum to carry himself backwards and forwards in time.

The rejection of maturity could hardly be more unlike Peter Pan's. Grass was not quite twelve when the war started. When he was fourteen, he was in the Hitler Youth. In 1944 he left his native Danzig as a soldier and, after being wounded, was taken prisoner by the Americans. He was still only seventeen when the war ended, but as he says himself, 'the experience of that short time had made me very ancient. I was still in my puberty, though, and this disharmony naturally had a strong effect on me in the years after the war'.

After working on a farm, in a potash mine, and as an apprentice to a firm that made gravestones, he became a student of sculpture and earned extra money as a drummer in a local jazz band. He also began to write poetry and plays, and for five and a half years – a tremendous amount of time to gamble

– he worked on *The Tin Drum*. Some of it is printed in dialogue form, and this is how he began to write it. 'Early on, in the middle fifties, I tried to write certain sections of it in play form. It didn't work, and as the years passed it became increasingly clear to me that it was material for a broad epic. But I didn't start on it till I was in Paris in 1956–7. I thought that this kind of narrative perspective, concentrated on a German province, could be of interest in Germany, but I never expected the rest of the world to be interested.'

The drumming obviously has roots in his experience of jazz, but the image of the dwarf derives from a visual conception which first surfaced in an unfinished poem. 'At the beginning of the fifties, when I was travelling around a lot as a student of sculpture, I wrote a longish poem from the opposite viewpoint. It was a lyrical-epical report by a young man who lives in a village, and one day he's had enough. He's a bricklayer and he builds himself a column in the village square, places himself on top of it, and so becomes a kind of modern saint on a column. From this elevated perspective he now describes everything that goes on around him. 'This position then turned out to be too static and I abandoned the poem. It wasn't any good anyway, but Oskar Matzerath is, if you like, a saint-on-the-column in reverse. From the perspective of the saint who looks at society from above came the idea for Oskar Matzerath, who peers over the edge of the table. Or sees underneath the table.'

As Grass sees it, Oskar's rejection of the adult world is paralleled by that of contemporary youth. 'There's a conspiracy to remain young, fear of age and fear of responsibilities. And what we're experiencing politically is deeply imbued with infantilism. For instance, President Nixon says America has never yet lost a war and it's his ambition to make sure she wins this one in Vietnam. I call that childish obstinacy. To be unable to understand a military defeat, which was already complete long ago, is a sure sign that an immature man – someone who hasn't understood how to become an adult – is President of the United States. And the consequence of having an infantilist at the head of a state can only be catastrophic.'

Local Anaesthetic, Grass's fourth novel and the first to be set
in the present, and the play *Davor*, which uses the same
characters and tells the same story, both focus on the Vietnam
war. The close relationship between play and novel is characteristic of the man who started to write his best novel as a play
and went on to work intensively in both media. 'I wrote *Local
Anaesthetic* and *Davor* parallel with each other. It's not as
though one was written first and then the other. I wrote the
middle section of the book twice, once as a play and once as a
continuation of the novel.'

That's a new way of working.

'Yes, finding it was a big stimulus for me, especially with
the changes I had to make in the dialogue. But I don't know
whether I'll ever work that way again.'

You no longer avoid flashbacks as you did in The Tin Drum.

'No, but they're not tiresome memory processes brought in
to move the story backwards and forwards. In *Local Anaesthetic*, the dentist has introduced a television set into his
surgery and my aim at least is to make everything objective!'

The television set is there to distract the patient, and the
pictures on the screen set his mind wandering through memories and fantasies. The central character is a seventeen-year-
old student who is distracted from protest by his need for
dentistry. Knowing how ineffectual it would be if he burned
himself to death in the Kurfürstendamm, Philipp Scherbaum
plans to set fire to his dog in front of one of the cafés where
ageing ladies sink their teeth into creamcakes. He will hold up
a poster saying 'This is petrol, not napalm'. The form-master,
Starusch, concerned at the consequences the gesture could
have for a promising pupil, tries to dissuade him, and succeeds
in passing on something of his own liberal confusion, while
the boy's intolerant girl-friend Vero prods at him impatiently.
'Mao warns us against the motley intellectuals.'

Grass's attitudes have something in common with the
teacher's but he was naturally disappointed to be equated with
him by so many of the German critics. 'Naturally, Starusch is
close to me, if only because he belongs to my generation, and
he inclines, like many people of that generation, to resignation.
Of course, I describe these attacks of resignation, but how I
deal with them myself, that's another story. I don't think I
incline towards resignation because I have no capacity for

enthusiasm. I've been so sceptical, right from the beginning, that my attitude is cheerful pessimism. Starusch battles with the schoolboy and finally achieves a questionable success – or partial success – but generally he's more aware of a direct trivial pain, like his toothache, than a stronger abstract pain, like the war in Vietnam, while his pupil, Scherbaum, is sensitive enough to be affected directly by an injustice which is as remote as that.

'The point about *Local Anaesthetic* that our critics hardly noticed was that it's a satirical novel. In Germany it was received with a great deal of sour seriousness and it was left to the foreign reviewers to respond to the desperate humour in the book – especially in the dentist. People missed the vision and the fantasy of *The Tin Drum* and *Dog Years*, but they're there in *Local Anaesthetic*, only in a different form, and adapted to the very trivial present. In *The Tin Drum*, *Cat and Mouse* and *Dog Years*, I was predominantly concerned with the past, especially the German past. All three books were oriented to great events – war, dictatorship, the collapse of the dictatorship, surrender, big troop movements – though all this was reduced down to Danzig and the petty bourgeois atmosphere. This phase of my work is provisionally finished. *Local Anaesthetic* is my first book about the present. The action is set during peacetime, with the Vietnam war only on the fringe of the plot. Scherbaum and Vero Lewand belong to a generation which has grown up in peacetime. The book's not about power politics but the impotent protest-gesture of burning a dog. That's the difference between the two kinds of material, and of course it's a very conscious engagement with the theme of peace, which offers very different tensions from war.'

The blurb of the English edition says the theme is 'the resignation of the middle aged to only rarely being able to influence the younger generation'.

'I wouldn't call it resignation, but there are limits to the possibility of communicating experiences one's had oneself. And limits to what can be taught. Every new generation insists on its right to have its own experiences and make its own mistakes.'

Grass has immersed himself actively in politics, canvassing energetically for Willy Brandt and the Social Democrats in the 1965 election campaign and again in 1969, though by then he had quarrelled publicly with Brandt, who had joined the coalition government under the ex-Nazi Kiesinger. In between the two campaigns, Grass became disillusioned with the 'classroom revolutionaries' who stop protesting when they marry and have to earn a living.

'Let me give you some examples. You can read in today's papers about the election of students' representatives at Cologne, a university with over 20,000 students. 38 per cent voted in the election. During the student troubles the figure went up to 60-65 per cent. It hasn't taken long for it to sink back to a very low level, which shows how apolitical attitudes begin while students are still at the university, concentrating short-sightedly on their exams and such things. Today when we speak about student protest, we're making the mistake of generalizing. It's only a proportion of students who are at all interested in politics, and, naturally, inside that group a small section has become radical. But it's an overall minority which gets involved in any political activity. The same is true of the schools. So it's nonsense to assume that in the aggregate the younger generation is far more political in its reactions than the older generation or than previous generations. What's more, the students and the high school children with their New Left principles are of course more privileged than the others. In school and in university they're in a protected position. Many of them are scared of leaving university because they know very well that their workaday life is about to begin and that compromises will be demanded of them. They have a presentiment – many of them have watched their elder brothers and sisters – that it's no longer going to be so easy to have absolute standards. So altogether, although it gets a good deal of sympathy, it's basically an infantile attempt to prolong childhood, to hold on to the status of irresponsibility.

'The more serious political consequence is the widening rift between the intellectuals and potential intellectuals with higher education on the one hand and the mass of the working-class population on the other. This is very ominous, as we can see in America, where a large part of the Trade Union movement, the "hard-hat" building workers for instance, may well continue their defence of Nixon's policies and go all out against "the intellectuals". We've seen similar signs here in Berlin at the time of the student troubles. But it's not the fault of the workers. At least, not entirely. When a left-wing student decides to work on the factory floor for three months to learn about capitalism's forms of oppression, as he calls them, the worker will be suspicious of that. The student will have the feeling "Now I'm one of the proletariat – for three months". But the worker is serving a life sentence, standing by his job, working at the conveyor belt. That's the irremovable difference. In *Local Anaesthetic* I try to clarify the basis of the struggle, to show where it begins – in school.

'Another point that hasn't been noticed by the critics is that there are two protest movements in *Local Anaesthetic*. The first happens in the middle of the 1950s – the protest of the former soldier Schlottau and his companions against the character Krings and against German rearmament, the "*Ohne mich*" movement, which was the protest of a generation that was fed up to the teeth with the war. This "without me" attitude is a refusal, an abstention, like many of the gestures of protest made today, which are also passive.'

Like Norman Mailer, Günter Grass has been trying to divide his life between literature and politics; unlike Mailer's, his writing has not veered down towards a journalistic level, but the personal strain has been enormous. 'When I'm working on a book, I disappear for several weeks or months. I go away three or four times a year and work on nothing but the book. Political activity is for me not like a solitary walk but a political orientation, which is to say an orientation towards the European working-class movement and its history, but especially towards the Social Democrats. All this has always been influenced by England, in a way that's never been sufficiently studied, particularly in relation to revisionism inside the Social Democracy. Eduard Bernstein was very deeply impressed by the Parliamentary tradition, and he spent many years in England. Engels, too, was deeply impressed by the early form of English Socialism and also by the pragmatic way conflicts could be resolved in England without letting absolute ideas distort the horizon, although many mistakes were made through the exclusively pragmatic way of marking time – through pragmatism, in fact. So, for me, it's not a question of entering into some form of political activity side by side with literature, but it relates to a strand of the European Enlightenment, a strand which is capable of political development. With all the fragmentation and cellular division that have gone on in them, Socialism as a whole and the European working-class movement belong to the Enlightenment. Inside this movement is German Social Democracy, which particularly interests me, and which, here in the centre of Europe, has achieved a moment of stability. The Social Democrats didn't want a war and didn't have to redeem a war. They are the permanent guarantee in Germany of what is still necessary – the development of democratic traditions.'

His own relationship with the SPD naturally changed when it finally won through to success at the polls. 'Precisely because it's now the government, my attitude has become more critical. There are two factors, the SPD's share in the government, the leading role we must play as a party, and the condition of the Party itself. Then there is a great deal to reform. Most members of the Party behave as they did before – as if they still had to live on the defensive, as an opposition party. They've not yet fully understood the consequences of having to take on the other democratic function – that of governing. The Party must now give a proper priority to the claim it has been making since 1959 – that it wants to become a people's party – through an opening of the Party, getting away from narrowness and reserve. That was the gist of my contribution to the SPD Party Conference at Saarbrucken.'

His shrewd realism is a refreshing force in a left wing which, throughout Europe, is prone to the sort of complacency and conformism that can lead to inaction in face of an opportunity which may never recur. In 1968, Grass was one of the first to realize what a great opportunity was lost in Czechoslovakia and how little was being done to support Dubcek. 'The European Left is too full of literary utopianism. There are too many writers who go out looking for a Utopia, side-stepping the difficulties on their doorstep. If they can't take Cuba as a model, then it has to be China, because it's so hard to know what's happening there. So they talk to you in detail about the horizon without noticing what's going on in front of them.

Many of them haven't understood that the Czechs were making the first serious attempt at de-Stalinization to be made anywhere and making it with reference back to Marx. The New Left is always appealing to the examples of China without realizing how badly it's slipping into Stalinism. And however critical the New Left imagines itself to be, it keeps going uncritically back to the concept of Marxism-Leninism, which is a contradiction in itself. The correct concept would have to be Leninism-Stalinism.

'The break from Marxism came with Lenin. What happened in Czechoslovakia, as the theoreticians knew and the vast majority of the population didn't, connects up with the defeat of the first demands that were made for a humanization of Socialism. Very early on, Rosa Luxemburg criticized Lenin and prophesied exactly what would happen – the departure of Lenin and Leninism from the basic requirements of Marxism. The New Left ignores this. To make a genuine start with de-Stalinization, the first sacrifice would have to be Lenin. If there had been no Lenin and no single-party system, if the separate Soviet Republics hadn't been deprived of all power, there could have been no Stalin. Social Democracy in Czechoslovakia had an excellent alternative to offer both to the East and the West. In the East it wasn't understood that with the help of Czech democratic Socialism, Communism could again become socially feasible. In the West there should have ben great excitement and a bridge could have been built. For the first time, the dogmatic tyranny of the Party was being challenged and with it the Soviet domination of the whole Eastern block.'

The play that Grass wrote in 1965, *The Plebeians Rehearse the Uprising*, focuses on another opportunity that was missed by the Left – in 1953 when workers in East Berlin rebelled against the government. 'I was in Berlin on the 16th and 17th June. My wife and I went over to East Berlin on the 17th. It was cordoned off but you could see something of it at Potsdamer Platz. The only foreign writer who understood the significance of 17th June was Camus. He saw that it was a workers' rising, not a popular rising. What was interesting was that he said this rising was one of the first signs that the Germans had conquered the Nazism in themselves.'

The play is about a playwright-director, unmistakably

modelled on Brecht, who is rehearsing *Coriolanus* with a company unmistakably modelled on the Berliner Ensemble while a rebellion is going on outside. 'The action tests the way his interest is divided between the technical problems presented by the plebeians in the play and the practical and moral problems presented by the workers who want him to help them.'

Clearly and cleverly, the play reflects Grass's unhappiness about Brecht's relationship with 'a political regime which contradicted his art and his ethic in everything it did. I always wondered how someone who took such a high revolutionary and humanistic line in his formulations could go along with such a blatant dictatorship.'

Could he have done anything practical against it?

'I don't know, but in any case he was a party to it and he was carried, exploited, promoted by this system. He had privileges within it and that makes many of his political statements questionable – perhaps unbelievable.'

And in your play 'The Plebeians Rehearse the Uprising' . . .

'Yes, it's true Brecht is the starting point but I'm also concerned in general with the difficulty of an intellectual who gets involved so critically with state authority and then has to confront the consequences of his decisions.'

If you'd been in this position yourself, you'd have had the same problems but you would have behaved differently?

'You know, no one can be sure of how he'd behave in a situation where his life is in danger, of how brave or how cowardly he'd be. But I believe the price Brecht paid for his undisturbed theatrical activity was too high, and I don't believe I'd have paid it. At least I hope not.'

Grass was born in Danzig – now the Polish town Gdansk – the son of a German grocer and a Slavonic mother. Danzig, as he says, was a modern port and a medieval town. The seagulls, the fish and the potato fields are brought vividly to life in *The Tin Drum* and *Dog Years*, and his descriptions seem to involve all the other senses three-dimensionally – taste, touch and smell. But what is even more remarkable is his capacity for unifying personal and political history in a bizarre comedy which flickers like lightning between reality and fantasy, illuminating vast tracts of territory beyond the range of any other contemporary writer.

He had been an altar boy in a Catholic church and later spent several of his formative years in the Hitler Youth. 'It's that time,' he says, 'that made me immune to ideologies.' Between the ages of sixteen and twenty he was a soldier in the German Army and then a prisoner in an American camp.

'Yes, but I wouldn't have missed those experiences. It's because of them that today I'm very quick to notice when for instance the language that the younger generation uses is still rational but the goal is irrational, though that's a tendency that's less marked in Germany than in America.'

His early life led him into an involvement with political events which has made them inseparable from his private life. 'Because I refuse to take politics or history unconditionally. Here in Germany we have to cope with the war and its aftermath. We can't wipe out the idea of a war which we started and lost. With the younger generation I notice a growing tendency to want to step out of history, to start again at zero. That is unhistorical and can only lead to catastrophe. Basically they're making the same mistake as their fathers, who in 1945 thought "Now, it's all over, now we can start again at zero". But there was no zero. There was an unconditional surrender, but that was the consequence of something. Like the situation today, it can only be explained in terms of a development which had its main sources not in the Nazi era at all, but in the Weimar Republic.'

Above all, Grass is a poet. 'Everything I've so far written has its origin and impulse in the lyrical.' And as Kurt Lothar Tank* has suggested, jazz rhythms have been an important influence. 'A studied monotony, exactly calculated displacements, and *pizzicati* passages are as characteristic of his work as is the disappearance and re-emergence of melody.'

Grass concedes this. 'Earlier on I played a lot of jazz, especially Dixieland music, as a drummer, and naturally that had a strong influence, which is still there, because musical forms are for me often a mode for literary forms – a rondo-

* *Günter Grass.* Frederick Ungar, New York, 1969.

like treatment of a theme, for instance, or strongly rhythmic writing.'

The other non-literary factor is the training Grass had as a sculptor. A metaphor can become the base for an intricate structure, elaborated playfully, but with painstaking concern for the relationships of shapes. 'My whole working discipline is really that of a sculptor. I know, as a sculptor, that when I alter one detail, one proportion, however insignificant, this will have consequences throughout the whole work. And as a sculptor I learned to see all round a subject. Many of these experiences translate into the writer's work.'

The seminal images in his early novels and early plays – *Flood*, *Onkel Onkel*, *The Wicked Cooks* and *Only Ten Minutes to Buffalo* – are mainly visual, the later novels and plays take a more dialectical form. 'That all developed out of *Dog Years*. That's where I started to work dialectically. I don't want to imitate myself and go on writing *The Tin Drum* all over again. I have to go forward, and I don't know where.'

MAGGIE SMITH and
ROBERT STEPHENS

❧⊙❧

The careers of Maggie Smith and Robert Stephens might have been very different – and less successful – if they had not been invited to join the company at the National Theatre for its opening season in 1963. She had done a season (1959–60) at the Old Vic, where Laurence Olivier saw her in Congreve's *The Double-Dealer*, and she worked with him briefly later in 1960 when she took over from Joan Plowright in Ionesco's *Rhinoceros*, but most of her experience had been in revues like *Share My Lettuce* (1957) and light comedies like Peter Shaffer's *The Private Ear* and *The Public Eye* (1962) or *Mary Mary* (1963). 'I think if I hadn't gone to the National when I did, I would have got into a comedy rut. I thought I was going to be in things like *Any Wednesday* and *Barefoot In The Park* for ever.' She was still in *Mary Mary* when the invitation came to play leading parts in Farquhar's *The Recruiting Officer*, *Othello* and *The Master Builder*. 'I got so windy I said no. Then sent a hysterical telegram saying yes. I don't know why. Just thinking about it and talking with friends. You know, someone saying "Oh don't be ludicrous! You can't possibly not play Desdemona with Larry playing Othello." But I think my reaction was everybody's reaction. They all thought the idea was absolutely insane. Which made it very difficult to play it, actually. Because it was so way out.'

Robert Stephens also felt inclined to refuse when he was offered Horatio in *Hamlet*, the National's opening production, and Captain Plume in *The Recruiting Officer*. 'Larry and Bill Gaskill came to the house and said "Would you like to join the National Theatre Company?" and I said "No, I don't want to do that". I'd always avoided classical companies. I thought "I can't bear them. I don't want to be stuck in one of these places, seeing the same faces day in and day out". But then John Dexter called up and said "Listen, John Neville has just dropped out of the Dauphin in *St Joan* at Chichester, so would you like to include that in the parts you'll be playing in the first season?" And that clinched it. I thought "Oh yes, that's a marvellous idea. I'm sure nobody else would ever cast me as the Dauphin". And so I agreed to go into the company.'

It was less of a switch of direction for Robert Stephens than for Maggie Smith. He had done a lot of work at the Royal Court during the first four years of George Devine's regime, starting as Judge Haythorne in *The Crucible*, the new company's second production, with Joan Plowright as Mary Warren and Alan Bates in the very small part of Hopkins. When Laurence Olivier accepted the position of Artistic Director of the new Chichester Festival Theatre, he opened in 1962 with a company that did not include many actors from the Royal Court, but in 1963, when one of the three productions (*St Joan*) was directed by John Dexter, the new company included Frank Finlay, Colin Blakely and Robert Stephens, who had all worked there. Then, after Olivier had appointed Dexter and William Gaskill – another director who had won his spurs at the Court – as his associates for the National, the company they recruited contained three elements: members of the Chichester company, actors who had been working mainly in the West End and actors from the Royal Court.

MAGGIE SMITH: It was a very good amalgamation of people.

ROBERT STEPHENS: John and Bill brought a good two-thirds of the company in with them. And Larry and Bill and John were a very good combination, because they were so totally different. Bill was a great intellectual. John Dexter was a very theatrical kind of character. And Larry – they always got on very well together. There was a constant sparking off. If it's all placid, it's dull.

They both enjoyed doing plays in repertoire rather than repeating the same performance eight times a week:

M.S.: It keeps one much more alive. It's the grinding it out night after night after night, and week after week after week that is much more taxing than anything else. But when you have a different play to do and different faces and different periods...

R.S.: Also it means you're constantly on your toes. You're always a bit nervous if you haven't done a play for a week – which gives it a charge of electricity. And sometimes we wouldn't do a play for twelve weeks. Then we'd simply have a word rehearsal before the performance and then do it. So constantly it was being revitalized because we hadn't become tired of it.

There is also less danger of forgetting whereabouts one is in a play:

M.S.: I remember these awful blank moments when you get 'I don't know what act I'm in', or 'Have I said that before?' or 'Is this the same night as last night?' It's very alarming when that awful *déjà vu* thing happens. You wonder where you are, or whether you've said that bit, or whether you haven't. That is when your concentration starts to go, which is disaster. And of course in repertoire you have to concentrate so much. You have to cling to it like mad.

R.S.: I think in the classical play – because the form of speech is different – you probably concentrate a bit more.

M.S.: Characters aren't quite so cardboard and camp, they're real people. And I think that's why they're such really charming plays. Particularly *Beaux' Stratagem* – it's about a very human situation.

Not that playing Noël Coward is easy. They made it seem effortless enough in 1964 when they played together in *Hay Fever* at the National, with Coward himself directing, and again in 1972, in the West End, when they played the leading parts in *Private Lives* under John Gielgud's direction. But, as Maggie Smith says, 'Verbally, one has to be very dexterous somehow. It's not as complicated, obviously, as a lot of plays, but it needs a lot of delicacy and accuracy. *Private Lives* is a deceptive play. It seems to be terribly simple, but it's not. It's weird. One just has to have the right touch.' She certainly had exactly the right touch for Amanda, winning huge laughs and even rounds of applause out of lines which look only mildly funny on the page, and delighting the audience with her smooth modulations between tired reasonableness and conscious outrageousness.

With *Hay Fever* she found that the balance of the play had altered. What was frightfully funny originally, wasn't funny in 1964, because people are used to theatrical families now. They read about them every day at breakfast. The Redgraves. But in 1925 it must have been alarming to see the way this actress behaved. When it was originally done it was the family that was frightfully funny, but in 1964 it was the visitors who were absolutely bizarre. Whereas I'm sure, originally, that they got very few laughs – they were the dreary bits in between.

R.S.: Well, the guests, taken at face value, are awfully dreary. A dull diplomat, a flapper, a dreary young man and an amateur boxer, and your part, which was just a sort of dizzy dame.

M.S.: Noël noticed how completely the balance had changed. But it says so much for the play that it could take the alteration. It enriched it, in actual fact.

R.S.: Also the play was written for a great star. It was tailored for her – including little songs she sings. Marie Tempest always sang a little French song in her plays. So the audience went to see Marie Tempest playing this retired actress.

M.S.: It's the same thing again with *Miss Julie* – that it's really no longer so startling for a lady to whizz off with the butler. So why all the fuss? It's odd, the way the balance goes in some plays.

Though Maggie Smith made her London debut in revue, she never had any training as a singer or dancer:

M.S.: I went to a drama school which was at Oxford, attached to the rep, the Oxford Playhouse. I worked more or less as a dogsbody – as an assistant-assistant stage manager, and understudied absolutely everybody under the sun. And I never *did* anything. But if you worked it cleverly enough at Oxford, you could do weekly rep round the colleges. The first thing I ever did was *Twelfth Night* for the Oxford University Dramatic Society. Then we started doing odd

revues and things like that. And actually I started on the
Fringe in Edinburgh doing late night revues in Riddle's
Court, which doesn't exist now. A terrible old room. And
I went up there for about three years, doing revues. And
then they transferred one from Edinburgh to the Watergate
Theatre, which is now no longer there. It was underneath
the Strand.

Even after she had joined the National, there was a danger that
she would not stay the course:

R.S.: After she had been in the National quite some time she
was prepared to leave, having made a success there. And she
still didn't quite believe it.

M.S.: I don't remember that.

R.S.: Well I do. I was called up one day by somebody who
said 'For God's sake you've got to convince her that she
ought to stay. Because she's thinking of leaving and going
back into the West End'. You think 'Oh actors are very successful and full of confidence', and so indeed she should have
been. But they're not.

M.S.: I think that confidence is a word that you can really
scratch right through for every actor in the world. Because
it seems to me that it gets less and less. It should build, but
it doesn't. Because it gets more and more difficult. I had
much more confidence when I first started than I have now.
You have a blind kind of confidence – you can't possibly go
wrong, its this insane youthful thing – when you start out.
You're whamming around with confidence and you don't
think at all. Of course the moment you realize exactly what
you're up against, it's very overwhelming, because it is a
frightfully difficult thing to do, to act in the way that you
really want to. You become terribly aware of the things that
you can't do and the way that one takes a fluff. You shirk
it. You get round it or you avoid it. Which is what happened, for example, with *Miss Julie*. But you find that you
can't go on doing that. You have to face the problem. Because if you don't, you're cheating everybody. You know
you are. And God knows, that line of Nina's in *The Seagull*
is right. 'You can't imagine what it feels like, when you

know you're acting abominably.' Which is what I feel, I'm afraid, far too frequently. But there you are.

You shirk automatically when you start. I mean you don't really want to know about the nasty sides of people, and what's going on. But with somebody like Ingmar Bergman you cannot avoid facing yourself, and you realize, 'Yes, I am capable of all these extremely unattractive thoughts and deeds'.

R.S.: Yes, I think that's a very strong feeling amongst 90 per cent of actors. They're simply frightened of examining those aspects of the characters. They feel that if they expose them, the audience won't like them as individuals. They think 'Yugh, how nasty!' I've seen it happen time and time again, especially with actresses, strangely enough. Middle-aged ones. If there's something bad about the lady they're playing, a mother or something, they simply will not do it. They say 'But she's a loving mother and cares for the children' and all that. Whereas Bill Gaskill says 'But don't you understand that if you show the other side, you make the character much more sympathetic?' You don't make her any more sympathetic by kicking it out and ignoring it.

M.S.: That's why it gets so complicated. There are so many facets to absolutely anything. You have to show every single possible bit.

They both found there was an extraordinary precision in the work of Ingmar Bergman, who directed them in *Hedda Gabler* at the National in 1970.

R.S.: His moves were very specific. There weren't that many moves in the production, in fact. It was very economical and when you had a move, it was almost to the millimetre. The positions were very strongly marked. You never got further than the point he wanted you to get to – the stage picture was always very set.

M.S.: I think that was what gave it that strange sort of filmic quality. You moved into a light, or you moved into focus. You moved into close-up, almost.

R.S.: He's the only director I've ever worked with who's used a screen technique in the theatre. Or a lot of screen techniques. Mostly movie directors direct movies and theatrical directors do plays, but he does both. I felt very strongly that he was using a kind of camera technique to bring people into sharp focus or into depth when they weren't that important.

M.S.: And one really depended on him entirely, because he was so sure. His conviction was so enormous, we were just swept along with it. I'm sure lots of people didn't agree with it, but that's too bad. And of all the productions that one has done there, I think that *Hedda* retained the same standard every night, somehow. Well, obviously it changed a bit – the chances are that they do change anyway. But somehow in that production there was a great unity to it all. The whole concept – everybody really believing in it. And there wasn't – as there so often is in plays – a sort of pacifistic 'Oh I don't like this bit that's coming up' or I'm never too sure of it and why didn't we try doing it another way?' We didn't seem to have any of that feeling. Often one does start readjusting and trying to change it and do different things.

The other director for whom they share an extremely high regard is William Gaskill, who directed them in the two successful Farquhar productions at the National, *The Recruiting Officer* (1963) and *The Beaux' Stratagem* (1970).

M.S.: They both had the same designer, but what one got out of them somehow was Bill's tremendous affection for the writer. They're curious plays because they're very domestic. With a lot of Restoration plays the plots are so dense and complicated that you get flummoxed. But the fans and the snuff-boxes don't exist in Farquhar at all, nor the frippery that usually goes on, and the beauty spots, and the camp, and the tapping each other, and the flouncing around. In Farquhar the characters are real people. I think that's why they're such really charming plays. Particularly *Beaux' Strat*. It's about a very human situation.

R.S.: Bill's very much like John Dexter in certain respects – in that he lays incredible stress on the text. I mean he makes you really examine it. Especially when we started *Recruiting Officer*. But with so many classical plays, a lot of the actors don't understand what they're saying. They can say it as though it makes sense, but in fact the audience doesn't always get the point of the arguments being put forward. Actors tend to say 'Well just do it quickly and then it'll be over'. But Bill's marvellous in that role. He really gets the absolute most out of the text.

During rehearsals of *The Recruiting Officer* Gaskill made the actors improvise and paraphrase the text:

M.S.: . . . sort of trying to say the text in your own words. I mean really making sure that you understand what you're saying. And we played different parts. So that you felt what it was like being the other person and saying their lines as well as listening to your own. I always find this very valuable, because another person can suddenly say something and you go 'Oh yes, of course, that makes sense'. Or 'I see that', or 'I see now why I have to answer so that you can almost get carried by it'.

R.S.: Other directors say 'Well, improvise' and it does far more harm, because the director doesn't quite know how to improvise to the point he wants. If you don't know that, you mustn't use improvisation. It frightens the actors to death. They don't know what the hell they're doing and they become totally confused. But Bill's whole point was that the improvisation was used so that the actors wouldn't leave anything out in their minds when they were playing speeches or scenes. So you could read a scene and then do it in your own words. And then he'd say 'But you left out that point and that point and that point. Now read it again'.

M.S.: Yes, you had to get all the points in your head.

R.S.: So in fact you knew the text in your own words. He said 'You'll find that you'll never dry, because you understand the pattern of the scene, the points of the scene, where you're going in the scene, and you know what you're talking about'.

If Bergman and Gaskill were the two directors from whom they learnt most while they were at the National, the experience of working with Olivier as an actor was also invaluable.

M.S.: The most difficult thing I had to overcome, I think, was the fact that I would veer automatically – I suppose I still do, and it's a fault – towards the comedy. Because it's somehow easier for me to do that.

But in *The Master Builder*, for instance, Olivier and she (playing Solness and Hilde Wangel) found a great deal of very useful comedy in lines that are usually played with a flat seriousness.

R.S.: I think it's a very good thing to do. There's the story about Larry – I don't know whether it's apocryphal – but whenever he was given a big, classical, tragic role to play like Coriolanus or King Lear, he immediately went through it to find out how many laughs there were.

M.S.: Well, you do need the laughs, I must say. I mean some of the plays are so heavy and turgid, like *Miss Julie* or *Hedda*. But if you, in your mind, see what's funny about them, you avoid the danger of getting the laughs in the wrong place. Which certainly happened when we first did *Miss Julie* at Chichester.

R.S.: The audience laughed, and Margaret was terribly upset about it. Mystified by it.

M.S.: It was terrible. But it was because we didn't rehearse it enough and because we didn't really find the comedy, which must be there somewhere. I know it's lying very deep in that one, but it must be there. You have to use it to release the audience because it's all too much for them to take, you know, this endlessly erotic woman hanging on.

R.S.: What was interesting was that much later we were doing *The Dance of Death*, and I did a tremendous amount of background work on the play, and I discovered that when *Miss Julie* was performed originally, the audience laughed, and the actress, indeed, was very upset. And she went to Strindberg and said 'This is terrible. They laughed at me'. And he said 'Don't you understand? That's what I want'.

M.S.: Yes, I suppose you think it must be a harrowing play. One didn't have the courage to make it funny then. Of course it's funny when she goes completely off her head and unhinges and talks about those castles for Ludwig in Bavaria.

I suppose if one were more courageous, it would be all
right. In Strindberg's work there are terribly heavy and
ghastly moments and one's got to learn to skate and be very
delicate with them, I think. And I think you can only do it
if you approach it at a wrong angle. I mean there are some
moments when you think 'Well, this part is really just so
awful, this particular passage, and I shall feel all right when
it's over'. And that's when you tend to slide round it and be
a bit evasive. I wouldn't do it that way now, I know. I think
I'd take my courage in both hands and not try to stop the
laughs or not try to stop the audience being embarrassed.
Because that was obviously what he intended.

There are comedians like Frankie Howerd, comedy actors like
Kenneth Williams and comedy actresses, like Edith Evans,
Geraldine MacEwan and Maggie Smith, who develop their
voices in such a way that some of the sounds they make seem
intrinsically and irresistibly funny – full-throated scoops of
mock-horror, outrage or affronted dignity. While this talent is
a most valuable asset, a performer with integrity is bound to
worry about the dangers of using it as a refuge and of becoming mannered.

M.S.: There are certain ways of saying something that automatically get you a laugh. What's difficult is to make sure
that the audience never makes a mistake and that you use
the comedy at the right moment so that it can be over and
done with. If you just happen to say one line wrongly one
night, you would probably get a laugh. It's a matter of
working out the balance, which is a very delicate one.

Playing Kurt to Laurence Olivier's Edgar in *The Dance of
Death*, Robert Stephens had the experience of watching a great
actor discovering and projecting a lot of comedy that would
normally be missed.

R.S.: When I was asked to play the part, everybody said 'Oh
for God's sake, don't. It's a terribly dreary part'. And I
thought 'Well how silly!' Because I don't think Strindberg
wrote bad parts. And one would be offered the opportunity
of seeing Laurence Olivier create an enormous part at very

close quarters. I'd acted with him in *Recruiting Officer*, but I hardly met him in that play. So I did it. At least I went the entire way through the rehearsals of the production and was a solid part of it. And so one knew the balance of the production and the balance of his performance. And I was never upset by any laughs he got in seemingly tremendously serious and dramatic scenes – serious for me, as I was the dupe of the play. There was a scene in which I was being absolutely crucified, and suddenly there was an enormous laugh. I think a lot of actors would have been very upset by this. They would think the whole thing had gone wrong, or that they were being made a fool of. But that was the way the production was balanced, and I thought it was marvellous and absolutely right. And certainly no laugh was ever got at my expense as an actor.

But Olivier is remarkable. There was one scene when he received some bad news on a ticker-tape and he had to wreck the room.* And he felt he wasn't getting it right, and he asked me what I thought was wrong in it. And I said 'Well, for what it's worth, I think you're doing it *continuously*, so it's not frightening or alarming. But if you split it, like morse code, the silences are as terrifying as the smashing of the bottles and the furniture. Because we don't know what you're going to do next'. And he said 'Yes, you're absolutely right. Thank you very much'. And did it. Olivier's tenacity is exemplary. He'll worry at a character like a dog with a bone to explore to the nth degree anything that he tries for the character. And you feel finally that if the play stopped at any point and somebody said 'What are you feeling now?' he'd be able to tell you absolutely. He never leaves anything to chance. Or gives up because it's too difficult. He'll always root his way through it. It gives him a supreme confidence. Because he knows exactly what he's doing and where he's going. Working with him was also a constant reminder of the necessity, for an actor, of being in good condition physically.

M.S.: He knew about Shakespeare, knew about speech, knew about the control, knew how much you had to breathe in

* This scene is described at length in Ronald Hayman: *Techniques of Acting* Methuen, 1969.

and out and how much breath you needed. Sheer physical things. I didn't realize until I saw Larry going through *Othello*, which was an enormous physical task for a theatre director, how *fit* you had to be. And it wasn't any good hoping that the voice was 'small but pleasing' or anything like that. There was so much more to it. It took me a very long time. I know it wasn't until about the last two weeks of *Othello* that I thought I'd got somewhere near it. I knew it wasn't right, but it was a damn sight better than when it started.

A role which alerted Robert Stephens to the importance of physical factors was Atahuallpa in Peter Shaffer's *The Royal Hunt of the Sun*.

R.S.: That was frightfully difficult. I thought they were mad to cast me in the part. In fact it's a very small part in the play, although it comes out looking like a great big one. There's not much actual dialogue and he doesn't really appear until the second half as anything important. And I thought 'What am I going to do? I've got to appear to be somebody quite extraordinary, outlandish and bizarre'. So over the ten weeks we rehearsed it I thought that the most important thing was the physical side of it. With a gymnast I worked terribly hard on making my figure look slightly different. And I thought 'The voice is very important', and we discovered that the Incas used to speak hitting consonants terribly hard and sighing away on some diphthongs, and we found that they were very influenced by birds, and made a lot of bird sounds. But it was a very gruelling thing to do, because there wasn't any picture of him in existence. Nothing to start with. Nobody knows anything about the Incas at all nor what kind of creature he was. So it was made up entirely from one's imagination. I thought 'It must be in terribly bold strokes, and if it's wrong then it's wrong, but at least it must be very strong'. I did a tremendous amount of research work on all sorts of things, to get some kind of character out of it.

A characterization like that of George Dillon in *Epitaph for George Dillon* by John Osborne and Anthony Creighton cost him relatively little effort.

R.S.: Joan Plowright said a very interesting thing, which I think is absolutely true: you work all your life on different parts and get no credit for it at all. And the one part that makes you a big success is probably the easiest that you'll ever play. Because it's probably so close to yourself. With her it was Beatie in *Roots*. It was not difficult for her to play that, because it was like her. With George Dillon it was easy for me. I knew John Osborne frightfully well. He's one of my greatest friends. The character was an unsuccessful actor-writer, so it was all the things that I knew. I was by no means successful so I identified with the character completely. I knew the way in which he spoke. And Ken Tynan in his notice said that I spoke very much like John Osborne himself, and indeed I did. I didn't copy him, but he writes very much as he speaks and one fell into it, naturally. Yes, I just heard the emphases and the cadences.

As he readily admits, Robert Stephens has a tendency to be over-relaxed physically, and when he was working at the Court he was more liable than he is today to let his spine go slack while moving about the stage. As Maggie Smith pointed out, it matters less in a small theatre. 'You can do a lot of things at the Court that you couldn't do on a big stage'. Playing Colonel Vershinin in *Three Sisters* he had to be careful not to use his body too much.

R.S.: Olivier said 'You can't do any of that. You musn't do just any gesture because the man is a *soldier*. But if you do use one, make it strong – he's used to handling cannons and guns. But don't use your hands at all if you can possibly help it. And you must never lean forward. You must always stand very stiff, because he's in the army and that's the way he's been brought up to stand'.

M.S.: The moment you move, you diffuse from whatever you're saying, though God knows, I'm the first to meander around and wander about. Sometimes it's valuable and sometimes it's dreadful. Because there are moments when you just have to be as still as possible to give clarity, which gets smudged when you start whirling around. Those are the mannerisms that one uses, as a comfort, a way out; you know that you can get over certain problems in a scene by chucking it about, fidgeting your way through it. If you're really honest, you just can't. You have to learn to live with yourself in repose.

Since *The Recruiting Officer* they have worked together a good deal, though never for very long at a stretch.

M.S.: I think of Robert as an actor when we're working and not as my husband. But I can see that it's easier for an audience to watch two people who are married playing two characters who are married. It's all done *for* you.

R.S.: There is obviously a naturalness, because you're not nervous that the other person might not quite like what you're doing or you're going too far or your breath may smell. But I'm always constantly surprised by Margaret. There are certain actors and actresses with whom you can never vary anything. You know them quite well but you just wouldn't dare. They don't like it. They like it to be always exactly the same, so they have it under control. But I wouldn't say that I knew beforehand the way in which Margaret was going to speak some line. I'm constantly dazzled by a different reading or a different approach to a line. I can't always say 'Well, I know exactly how she's going to play this, so I'll play my next line like that'.

ACKNOWLEDGMENTS

Most of the interviews on which these chapters are based were originally done for *The Times*, and shorter versions of them appeared on the Arts Page. I am grateful to the Editor for permission to incorporate this material and I should also like to express thanks to John Higgins, the Arts Editor, who commissioned me to do them in the first place.

The interview with David Storey was done for *Drama*, and I am grateful to its Executive Editor, Walter Lucas, both for commissioning it and allowing me to use it again. Part of the Scofield interview appeared in *Theatre 71* edited by Sheridan Morley and published by Hutchinson, so I am thankful to them for permission to use this material. The interview with Lord Olivier has not appeared in any other form.

Part of the Günter Grass interview appeared in *Encounter* and I am grateful to the Editors for permission to reprint this material.

Obviously I am grateful to all my subjects for giving me the interviews and I am especially indebted to those who have taken additional time to help me in preparing their section of this book.

Finally, I should like to thank Christine Bernard, whose editorial help has been invaluable.